Cuba, the Media, and the Challenge of Impartiality

Cuba, the Media, and the Challenge of Impartiality

by SALIM LAMRANI

Translated by Larry R. Oberg

Foreword by EDUARDO GALEANO

MONTHLY REVIEW PRESS

New York

Library of Congress Cataloging-in-Publication Data

Lamrani, Salim.
[Cuba, les midias face au difi de l'impartialiti. English]
Cuba, the media, and the challenge of impartiality / Salim Lamrani ;
translated by Larry R. Oberg ; foreword by Eduardo Galeano.
pages cm
Includes bibliographical references and index.
ISBN 978-1-58367-471-0 (pbk.) — ISBN 978-1-58367-472-7 (cloth) 1. Pams
(Madrid, Spain) 2. Cuba—Press coverage—Spain. 3. Spanish
newspapers—Objectivity. 4. Journalism—Objectivity—Spain. I. Title.
PN5319.M33P355 2015
070.4'4997291—dc23
2014039552

Typeset in Minion Pro 11/14

Monthly Review Press
146 West 29th Street, Suite 6W
New York, New York 10001

www.monthlyreview.org

5 4 3 2 1

Contents

*In memory of Maximilien Robespierre, our Liberator,
who still makes the powerful tremble.*

Smuggle out the truth, pass it through all the
obstacles that its enemies fabricate; multiply, spread by all
means possible her message so that she may triumph; through
zeal and civic action counterbalance the influence of money and
the machinations lavished on the propagation of deception.
That, in my opinion, is the most useful activity and the
most sacred duty of pure patriotism.
—MAXIMILIEN ROBESPIERRE

Foreword

by Eduardo Galeano

FIDEL CASTRO. HIS ENEMIES SAY that he was a king without a crown and that he confused unity with unanimity.

And in this sense his enemies are right.

His enemies say that if Napoleon had possessed a newspaper like *Granma* the French would have been unaware of the disaster of Waterloo.

And in this sense his enemies are right.

His enemies also say that, being more accustomed to echoes than to voices, he exercised power by speaking much and listening little.

And in this sense his enemies are right.

But his enemies do not say that in order to ensure his place in history he deliberately exposed his chest to bullets when the invasion occurred; or that he faced hurricanes as an equal, hurricane to hurricane; or that he survived six hundred and thirty-seven attempts on his life; or that his contagious energy was a decisive factor in transforming a colony into a country; or that it was due to a spell cast by a mandinga or a miracle of God that this new country was able to stand up to ten presidents of the United States who, with bibs tucked under their chins and knives and forks at the ready, were prepared to carve it up.

And his enemies do not say that Cuba is a bizarre country because it refuses to compete in the World Cup doormat competition. And they do not say that this revolution, which grew in punishment, is what it could be and not what it wished to be.

Neither do they say that, for the most part, the wall that separates desire from reality has continued to grow because of the Imperial blockade, which has stifled the development of Cuban-style democracy, which in turn has forced the militarization of the society and provided the bureaucracy—an entity that for each solution manages to find a problem—the alibis it needs to justify and perpetuate itself.

And they do not say that in spite of everything, in spite of external aggression and internal injustices, this island, which suffers but remains stubbornly cheerful, has generated the least unjust society in Latin America.

And his enemies do not say that this feat is the result of the sacrifices of the people. Nor do they say that it is the result of the stubborn will and the code of honor, something that harkens back to another era, of this gentleman who has always fought for losers, like his famous colleague from the countryside of Castile.

Introduction

A FREE AND INDEPENDENT PRESS and its corollary, a duty
to provide truthful information to all citizens, are essential to
any democracy. The media, moreover, are considered to be the
fourth branch of government, along with the legislative, execu-
tive and judicial and thus contribute to the stability of society.
The media can, however, only fulfill their role if they succeed
in emancipating themselves, not only from political powers, but
also from the power of money. At present, the phenomenon of
media concentration in the hands of economic and financial
powers has become, throughout the West, an undeniable reality. In France, two multinationals—Dassault and the Lagardère
Group—whose main activity is the international sale of weapons
and whose stock in trade is war—control the world of press and
publishing. Dassault alone controls more than seventy newspapers and magazines and Lagardère nearly fifty.

The challenge facing the media in Western societies is, therefore, one of size. Under these circumstances how can television
news, radio, print, or digital media deal impartially with the factual reality of transmitting complete and non-biased information
informing public opinion without going up against the interests of
the financial conglomerates that own them, whose sole purpose

is to maintain the established order? Is the mission of the press to provide objective information to citizens or is it to preserve the existing political, economic, and social order? Is it to defend a plurality of opinions or to impose an ideological framework aimed at preventing original and heterodox thinking? Should it present all points of view or censor and misinform when doctrinal barriers erected by the authorities are breached?

Cuba is the object of this study. The analysis of media discourse concerning this country is a revealing and fruitful exercise in that it is of ideological as well as media concern. Since the triumph of the Revolution and the rise to power of Fidel Castro, this small nation has been the subject of criticism and controversy. There is a reason for this: the process of transformation initiated in 1959 called into question the society's social order and its established structures. It challenged the powers that be and offered an alternative that, for all of its faults, all of its imperfections, and all of its contradictions, should not be underestimated. It proposed that the power of money no longer reign supreme and that available resources be allocated to the majority of citizens, not simply to a minority. How, therefore, can one describe Cuban reality in all its complexity when media owners subscribe to Voltaire's maxim that "a well-organized society is one in which the few govern and the many work to nourish them?" Despite its claims of impartiality, the press most often promotes a point of view and judgments that are generally negative toward Cuba, while relegating balance and nuance to the background in any debate over ideas.

This book, therefore, proposes to study how the media presents the Caribbean's largest island for public scrutiny. Its aim is to demonstrate the ideologically selective nature of the information posted on Cuba and how doctrinal censorship works when the facts contravene the dominant editorial line. The Spanish daily newspaper *El País*, whose viewpoint is pervasive throughout the Western press, will serve as reference.

EL PAÍS

Founded May 4, 1976 by José Ortega Spottorno at the beginning of the Spanish transition to democracy and six months after the death of Generalissimo Francisco Franco, *El País* gradually became the Spanish newspaper of reference for the progressive sector of the Iberian nation, in comparison to its conservative rival *ABC*. With a circulation of nearly 500,000 copies, it is the most widely distributed mainstream daily in the Iberian Peninsula. It also publishes a special edition aimed at Latin America and the United States.[1] The newspaper belongs to the Grupo PRISA,[2] the largest Spanish media consortium, which is a leader in the U.S. Hispanic market and, with a presence in twenty-two countries, a world leader as well.[3]

El País, much like the *New York Times*, is not only an opinion leader in the Spanish-American world but also around the globe. This status implies a great responsibility vis-à-vis public opinion. It requires the newspaper to be irreproachable and that it respect scrupulously the journalistic code of professional ethics. This code holds that "critical thinking, truthfulness, accuracy, integrity, fairness and impartiality are the pillars of journalistic action" and points to "accusation without proof, maliciousness, alteration of documents, misrepresentation, misappropriation of images, lies, manipulation, censorship and self-censorship and non-verification of facts" as the most egregious of professional abuses.[4]

The newspaper also has its own code of ethics, according to which *El País* is committed to "presenting information on a daily basis that is truthful, complete, interesting, current and of high quality in order to help readers understand reality and form their own opinions."[5] The newspaper states that its "independence and its non-manipulation of information guarantee the rights of readers, whose protection is the raison d'être of its professional work."[6] *El País* "provides readers with verified information, and refrains from including personal opinions."[7] Finally, the code emphasizes that "it should provide the reader with all data necessary for understanding the context surrounding the facts being reported."[8]

This study aims to analyze how Cuban reality is reflected in *El País* in light of the case of Mauricio Vicent and the subsequent criticism leveled against the Spanish daily. Indeed, on September 4, 2011, Cuba's International Press Center (IPC), affiliated with the Ministry of Foreign Affairs, decided against renewing the press credentials of Spanish journalist Vicent, a correspondent for *El País* and the radio station *Cadena Ser*. The IPC explained its decision to end Vicent's professional activity by invoking Article 46 of Resolution 182 of 2006 regulating the activities of the foreign press. The letter states that Vicent "violated journalistic ethics and was not objective in his publications." He is accused of transmitting "a biased and negative picture" of Cuban reality. Today, the Iberian reporter is allowed to visit the island but can no longer practice his profession in an official capacity.[9]

Present in Cuba since 1991, following the collapse of the Soviet Union, Vicent was one of the most senior foreign press correspondents stationed in Havana. His father, Mauricio Vicent Sr., was a left-wing journalist who also worked for *El País*. The admiration he felt for the Cuban Revolution led him to ensure his son's education, who ultimately earned a degree in psychology at the University of Havana. Married on the island and the father of two children, the younger Mauricio Vicent is close to most Cuban journalists, including those who work in an official capacity for state television. He has the reputation of being a connoisseur of Cuban reality.[10]

El País reacted virulently to the Cuban authorities' decision, denouncing it as "an attack on freedom of expression," stating that its "Havana correspondent's coverage is an exemplar of professionalism, impartiality and balance." The Madrid daily also denounced "the inability of the Cuban regime to understand the role of media, especially foreign media." Finally, it reaffirmed its "commitment to continue to report Cuban reality with the same rigor, the same respect and the same independence" it has shown up until the present.[11]

Faced with these two contradictory positions, an analysis of *El País*'s media coverage of Cuban reality will shed some light on this situation. Of course, all foreign correspondents, wherever they may be stationed, respond to an editorial line imposed upon them by their editors; indeed, sometimes against their will. According to certain Spanish, Cuban, and U.S. sources, this seems to have been the case for Mauricio Vicent. Thus the critical analysis that follows concerns the editorial policies of *El País* and the management responsibilities of the Grupo PRISA, the entity responsible for the approach taken by the newspaper. As the author of most of what was written about Cuba in *El País*, the journalist Mauricio Vicent cannot avoid his share of responsibility even if, as it would appear, he was merely doing the bidding of others. Indeed, the Spanish journalist Carlos Tena, his friend for some thirty years, reports that Vicent confessed to him that he was obliged to respect the editorial line imposed by his superiors: "If one day I were to write something positive about this country, they would fire me without hesitation."[12]

Eight issues concerning this case will be explored in this book. After tracing the ideological shift of *El País* in recent years, this study will focus on daily life in Cuba, the level of human development on the island, the issue of human rights, internal opposition, the case of dissident blogger Yoani Sánchez, the case of the five Cuban political prisoners held in the United States, the Alan Gross affair, and migration issues.

"The press is a school that serves to turn men into brutes because it relieves them of the obligation to think," wrote a disillusioned Gustave Flaubert in a letter to George Sand in 1871.[13] This book on the role of the media in our society aims instead to stimulate discussion of a fourth estate that exceeds its prerogatives in order to protect moneyed interests at the expense of its primary duty, which is to inform.

1

The Ideological Shift of *El País*

LONG CONSIDERED THE NEWSPAPER of reference in Spain and Latin America, the daily *El País*, reputed to be center-left, has in recent years undergone a spectacular ideological shift. It has adopted an editorial line that is conservative and particularly hostile to leftist Latin American governments in general and Cuba in particular, this to the point of competing with the Miami daily, *El Nuevo Herald*, a paper that represents the interests of the extreme right of the Cuban exile community.

It should also be noted that *El País* signed a trade agreement in March 2011 with *El Nuevo Herald* and is now distributed in Miami as a supplement to the Florida paper. This is an alliance that was concluded with the utmost discretion.[14]

Two editorials, written ten years apart, are emblematic of the ideological right turn taken by *El País*. In 1997, on the occasion of the thirtieth anniversary of the death of the guerrilla Ernesto Che Guevara and the repatriation of his remains from Bolivia to Cuba, the newspaper published an ecstatic editorial review:

> Thirty years after the death of Ernesto Guevara—the most iconic and captivating of Cuban revolutionary guerrillas, the memory of whom has created both nostalgia for lost idealism

and a commercial bonanza for those who exploit his image, . . . The revolutionary figure of Che remains a symbol of the steadfast idealist and the man of action. . . .

Che returns: an event that provokes melancholy for faded ideals in those who were young progressives when Guevara, Fidel and Cienfuegos (the young "barbudos") were struggling. This is useful information for those who did not experience this period of the Cuban revolution and have known the Guevarist mythology only as an abstract evocation of a struggle for a better, more egalitarian and humane world. . . .

In the late 1950s and early '60s this was an anti-imperialist and subversive armed movement that ended the dictatorship of Batista and attempted to spread, through guerrilla deployment, egalitarian uprisings throughout Latin America.

Che was 39 years old and his political preoccupation, that of exporting revolution, became a myth. His image, multiplied around the world on hundreds of thousands of posters, became a badge of honor for many young people who saw in this asthmatic doctor the archetype of the heroic guerrilla who struggles for the betterment of humanity.

The third world, a concept that was prevalent at that time, meant, on the one hand, the most brazen denunciation of international imperialism for its exploitation and misery, but on the other, held out the promise of insurgencies that would transform the world.

Such a utopia has virtually ceased to exist. Only a few rebel nuclei remain in the world, four or five guerrilla groups in Latin America, a residue without a future in a world characterized today by the triumph of globalization and a harsh and uncompromising liberalism.[15]

However, on October 10, 2007, the occasion of the fortieth anniversary of the death of Che Guevara, *El País* published a particularly scathing editorial in which he was no longer portrayed as a guerrilla, but rather as a "caudillo":

In fact, his willingness to give his life for his ideas masks a darker purpose: a willingness to simply eradicate those who do not share his beliefs. Ernesto Guevara, Che, the fortieth anniversary of whose death in the Bolivian village of La Higuera is being celebrated, belongs to the grim saga of tragic heroes. These heroes are still present in terrorist movements of all kinds, from nationalist to jihadist, their condition as assassins, concealed in the martyr's shroud, propagates old prejudices inherited from romanticism.

Their plans and their examples have left nothing more than a trail of failure and death, not only in one place where they have triumphed, Castro's Cuba, but also in places where they have not achieved victory, from the Congo of Kabila to the Bolivia of Barrientos. This accounting, of course, does not include the many countries in which thousands of young people who wished to follow the example of this reckless myth were engaged in a chimerical adventure, the aim of which is to create the "new man" through the barrel of a gun.

Seduced by a "guerrilla nucleus" strategy, one aimed at creating many Vietnams, the only contribution Guevara and his Latin American policy supporters were able to serve up were new alibis that served to justify the authoritarian tendencies that were germinating on the continent. Faced with Che's armed challenge, military dictatorships have managed to present themselves as the lesser of two evils, if not as an inexorable necessity in the face of similar military dictatorships, such as that of Castro.

The fact that Che gave his life, and sacrificed the lives of many others, does not make his ideas better, particularly when we take into account the fact that one of the world's most totalitarian systems served as their incubator.

Given the context from which he emerged, the figure of Ernesto Guevara represents an updated version of Latin American "caudillism." He was a kind of armed adventurer who came up with new social ideals for the continent that, while not the ideals of colonial liberation, were to be achieved through the same means his predecessors had used. During the four decades that have transpired since his death, the Latin American left and, of course, its European counterpart, have completely rejected his objectives and his fanatical methods.[16]

Thus, in the space of a decade, Ernesto Guevara, in the eyes of the newspaper *El País*, went from being an "undeviating idealist," a symbol of the "struggle for a better, more egalitarian and humane world," an "example of the heroic guerrilla fighting for humanity's sake" and someone offering the "promise of fomenting a movement that would transform the world," to being a "murderer" who belonged to the "sinister saga of the tragic hero still present in terrorist movements of all kinds," a "caudillo," someone committed to "fanatical methods," a purveyor of "totalitarian ideas," and someone whose legacy has left a "trail of failure and death."

When one reads these two editorials, the first question that comes to mind is: What crimes did Che commit during that fateful decade, wherever he might have been, that need be called out in this manner? The ideological shift of the newspaper, in reality, may be explained through the emergence of a new Latin America that has brought to power leftist leaders in Venezuela, Bolivia, Ecuador, Nicaragua, Brazil, Argentina, and Uruguay.

The Spanish daily struggles against the accusation that it presents a biased picture of Cuban reality. Instead, it asserts that these "accusations . . . are completely false and reveal only that Havana . . . hopes to see the media behave as mouthpieces subservient to official Cuban discourse and not as witnesses to reality." *El País* maintains that it always presents "truthful and nuanced information."[17] It is now important to evaluate this assertion thematically.

2

Daily Life in Cuba

ACCORDING TO *EL PAÍS*, "After half a century of revolution, Cuban leaders cannot continue to blame external forces for the political, economic and social failure into which they themselves have precipitated the island."[18] The reader may be surprised at such a harsh judgment and see it as more worthy of the political opposition to the Havana government that emanates from the White House or the dissident community rather than impartial, fact-based journalism.

It is now appropriate to compare the paper's assertions to the facts on the ground. Cuba's economic difficulties are undeniable; anyone who has visited the island quickly realizes that though the extreme misery prevalent throughout the rest of the continent does not exist here, the poverty of the people is nonetheless real.

Contrary to what the Madrid newspaper asserts, however, the Cuban leaders, far from evading personal responsibility, clearly recognize the flaws in how the current system operates. To appreciate this, one needs only to quote President Raúl Castro, who spoke about this problem in December 2010, before the Cuban parliament: "Either we solve our problems or we fail after having for too long skirted the precipice."[19] Two years later he added: "It is essential to breach the colossal psychological barrier that results in a mentality rooted in the habits and concepts of the past."[20]

Regarding the monthly income of Cubans, Raúl Castro has demonstrated considerable insight: "Salaries are still clearly insufficient to meet all needs, and they have virtually ceased to fulfill their role, that of ensuring the socialist principle 'from each according to his ability, to each according to his work.' This has encouraged a lack of social discipline."[21]

Nor has Raúl Castro evaded the problem of corruption: "Faced with violations of the Constitution and the rule of established law, there is no alternative other than that of using the public prosecutor's office and the courts. This, in fact, is something we have already begun to do. We do it in order to demand accountability from offenders, whoever they may be, because all Cubans, without exception, are equal before the law."[22] Aware that corruption does not spare senior officials, he sent a clear message to leaders in all sectors: "We must put an end to lies and deception in the conduct of managers at all levels."

More solemnly, he relied on two of the Ten Commandments to clarify his remarks: "Thou shalt not steal" and "Thou shalt not lie." He also referenced the three ethical and moral principles of the Inca civilization, "Do not lie, do not steal, do not be lazy," which, he maintained, "should guide the conduct of all leaders of the nation."[23]

In 2005, Fidel Castro himself had denounced corruption in Cuba: "This country can auto-destruct, this revolution can destroy itself. . . . We can destroy it, but if we do it will be our own fault."[24] President Raúl Castro also castigated the lack of critical debate in Cuba by denouncing secrecy, complacency, and mediocrity, and calling for more openness. "Do not fear differences in the assessment of criteria and opinion. . . . Differences will always be preferable to a false unanimity based on simulation and opportunism. The possibility of critical debate is, moreover, a right that should be denied to no one." Castro denounced the excesses of the "culture of secrecy that [Cubans have] used for more than fifty years" in order to hide errors, failures, and shortcomings. "It is essential that we change the mindset of managers as well as that of all of our compatriots," he added.[25]

Raúl Castro made the following remarks to the Cuban media:

> Our press has spoken enough of the successes of the Revolution, and we have done the same in our discourses. But we must now go directly to the heart of our problems. . . . I am a fervent advocate for ending the culture of secrecy because this is the "magic curtain" that masks our shortcomings as well as hiding those individuals invested in maintaining the status quo. I remember that certain criticisms, which I supported, appeared in the press a few years ago. . . . Our bureaucracy was immediately set in motion and began to protest, arguing that "these criticisms do not help because they demoralize the workers." Indeed, which employees will be demoralized? Similarly, at The Triangle, a large state dairy in the province of Camagüey, the milk produced was fed to pigs in the region for a number of weeks simply because the tanker truck used to transport it had broken down. I asked a secretary of the Central Committee to denounce this situation in *Granma*. Some people came to see me to tell me that this kind of criticism was counterproductive because it demoralized workers, etc, etc. But what they did not know was that I was the source of the criticism.[26]

On August 1, 2011, during his closing speech before the Seventh National Assembly of People's Power, Cuba's parliament, Raúl Castro reiterated his remarks concerning the need for critical and open debate within the society: "All opinions should be analyzed, and when there is no consensus the differences should be brought to the attention of a higher authority allowed to make a decision; moreover, nobody has the authority to prevent this."[27] He called for an end to "the habit of complacency, self-satisfaction, and formalism that we see in the treatment of the national news." He stated that television and radio should begin to generate written materials and programs that, by their content and style, capture the attention of the public and stimulate debate in order "to prevent media coverage from being boring, improvised, and superficial."[28] Similarly, sectarian excesses have been strongly condemned by Raúl Castro. He denounced on television certain violations of religious freedoms that have occurred due to the intolerance "still rooted in the minds of many leaders at all levels."[29] He spoke of the case of a woman, a Communist Party cadre, whose career had been exemplary but who was nonetheless removed from her position in February 2011 because of her Christian faith. Her salary was reduced by 40 percent, in direct violation of Article 43 of the 1976 Constitution that prohibits any kind of discrimination. The President of the Republic denounced "the harm caused to a Cuban family by attitudes based on an archaic mentality, fueled by deceptiveness and opportunism." Recalling that the victim of the discrimination was born in 1953, the year of the attack on the Moncada barracks carried out by supporters of Fidel Castro against the Batista dictatorship, Raúl Castro stated:

> This is not why I went to the Moncada. . . . I brought up this matter at the 30th of July meeting, the one that marked the 54th anniversary of the assassination of Frank País and his faithful companion Raúl Pujol. I had known Frank in Mexico and I saw him again in the Sierra. I do not remember having known a soul as pure as his, as courageous, as revolutionary, as noble and humble. Speaking to one of the leaders of the group responsible for this injustice having been committed, I said to him, "Frank believed in God and he practiced his religion, something I know he never ceased to do. So what, in this case, would you have done to Frank País?"[30]

On productivity and economic policy, the most senior leaders, starting with Raúl Castro, recognize both "a lack of economic literacy among the population" and the mistakes of the past. "We do not think that copying someone else is a good choice, because doing so has caused us many problems in the past and, in the bargain, we copied poorly."[31] Everyone now admits publicly that "spontaneity, improvisation, superficiality, the non-fulfillment of objectives, the lack of depth in feasibility studies and the lack of a comprehensive vision when undertaking an investment" are causing serious harm to the nation.[32]

Similarly, Raúl Castro has not hesitated to point out the negative effects of the ration book (*libreta de abastecimientos*), in force since 1960, including "its harmful egalitarian character," which became "an unbearable burden for the economy and failed to stimulate work productivity, while generating various illegalities in society." He also pointed to the following contradictions: "Given that the book was developed to serve more than 11 million Cubans equally, absurd examples of its failure to do so abound. For example, newborns are included in the distribution of coffee. Similarly, until September 2010 cigarettes were provided for both smokers and non-smokers, thereby encouraging the growth of an unhealthy habit in the population." According to the Cuban president, the *libreta* "essentially contradicts the distribution principle that ought to characterize socialism, which is, 'from each according to his ability, from each according to his work.'" For these reasons, it "will be important to implement measures aimed at eradicating the profound distortions in the functioning of the economy and society as a whole."[33]

Raúl Castro also acknowledged the need to "reduce excess staff in the state sector" and to put an end to the "confusion and improvisation that exist." Similarly, he said, "The mentality of inertia should be permanently banned in order to untie the knots that bind the development of productive forces," and noted that it is essential to find "an effective antidote to the widespread mania for holding meetings."[34]

He denounced "bureaucratic obstacles." The Cuban press, which had long evaded the subject, no longer hesitates to denounce indolence, inefficiency, and abuse. *Granma*, the principal daily newspaper in the country and the official voice of the Cuban

Communist Party, virulently condemned government bureaucracy and, in an article entitled "Bureaucracy, from the Rule to the
Exception" called for "a change in the prevailing mentality," stating
that "there are still those who close their eyes to the new economic
and social scenario that is being put in place." Numerous officials
"have bureaucracy in their veins, appear to have been inoculated
with this deadly virus, enjoy their daily eight hours as execution-
ers who make life impossible for our citizens," and have no wish to
change "a system that erects barriers with impunity and demands
a fine or a bribe before any process can be resolved." *Granma*
called on the government to put an end to this "parasitic scourge
in public administration," notably through the implementation of
new measures that would expand the private sector.[35]

The daily *Juventud Rebelde* also denounced the "autocratic
methods and hierarchical organization" of a bureaucracy insensi-
tive to the problems of the population. The newspaper denounced
its "unforgivable and paradoxical" behavior, especially during this
time of great change in Cuba. It criticized a bureaucracy that does
not deign to respond to letters from citizens in more than 30 percent of cases and refuses "to assess the root problems. . . . Another
element of concern is the impunity with which the laws, standards,
and even the rights of citizens are violated before the very eyes of
senior executives."[36]

Alfredo Guevara, the father of Cuban cinema and a personal
friend of Fidel Castro, has approved the move to reform the government and has called for an end to the excessive nationalization
of Cuban society. "We are going through a process of eradication
of the nationalized society and out of this process I hope we will
construct a state that imposes limits on its functions and permits
the country to develop."[37] This will allow us to achieve "a level of
independence and maturity, something that will make a significant
contribution" to our society. Guevara himself often denounced the
Cuban bureaucracy as "absurd and inefficient"[38] and criticized
counterproductive state paternalism as well: "Our bureaucracy is
populated with administrators who think their only job is to give

orders. While the state is not the same as the bureaucracy, it is obvious that a disproportionately large state apparatus creates the phenomenon of ideologically based bureaucracy."[39]

The Cuban president highlighted two critical issues for Cuba: generational change and a lack of diversity. He denounced "the lack of systematic organization and political will needed to promote women, blacks, mestizos, and youth to positions of responsibility on the basis of merit and personal qualifications." He expressed his anger without evading his own responsibility: "To not have solved this problem in more than half a century is a shame we will have on our consciences for many years to come." Furthermore, Cuba suffers "the consequences of not being able to count on a reserve of talent properly prepared and with sufficient experience and maturity to assume the new and complex tasks of leadership in the Party, state, and government."[40] By way of example, the Central Committee of the Cuban Communist Party is composed of 115 members, including 48 women (41.7 percent) and 36 black or mixed race people (31.3 percent).[41]

Thus there is a serious disconnect between the premises of the Madrid daily and factual reality. Moreover, it is curious that though *El País* claims to present "truthful and nuanced information" and presents itself as an exemplar of journalistic "rigor," "professionalism," and "balance," it does not mention for a single moment the main obstacle to the economic development of the country: the economic sanctions imposed by the United States since 1960. Since 1992, those sanctions have been universally condemned by the international community. How can one evoke the daily difficulties of life in Cuba without mentioning the dramatic impact of the state of siege imposed by the United States and now in force for more than half a century?[42]

Certain facts allow us to grasp the scope of this problem. Since the imposition of total economic sanctions in 1962, Cuba has been prohibited from importing anything from the United States except for certain food products, and those only under the most draconian conditions. At the same time, the United States is the natural and historical market for the island because of its geographical location and, additionally, because it is the world's largest market. It should be recalled that in 1959, at the moment of the triumph of the Cuban Revolution, 73 percent of Cuba's exports were to the United States and 70 percent of its imports came from there.[43]

It is also necessary to examine the reasons why the Spanish newspaper ignores the extraterritorial economic sanctions levied against Cuba. Since the adoption of the Torricelli Act in 1992, the Helms-Burton Act in 1996, and the new restrictions imposed by the Bush administration in 2004 and 2006, trade with third countries has been affected greatly. Since 1992, foreign ships—Spanish ships, for example—that dock in Cuban ports are denied entry to the United States for a period of six months. This generates significant additional costs for Cuba, which depends mainly on shipping because of its insularity. It also forces the country to pay well above the market price in order to convince international carriers to deliver goods to the island. Similarly, since 1996, foreign entrepreneurs investing in Cuba on land nationalized in 1959 risk having their assets in the United States frozen. Moreover, since 2004, any automaker, regardless of nationality, must demonstrate to the Treasury Department that its products do not contain even a single gram of Cuban nickel in order to be able to sell on the U.S. market. It is the same for all food companies wishing to invest in the U.S. market. Danone (Dannon in the United States), for example, must demonstrate that its products contain no Cuban sugar. These retroactive and extraterritorial measures deprive the Cuban economy of considerable capital and deprive Cuban exports of many markets around the world.[44]

It is also surprising that El País does not wonder about the reasons for the persistence of the siege—something that is universally condemned, even by American public opinion—two decades after the end of the Cold War, though the United States maintains trade relations with China, Vietnam, and North Korea.

Thus, as is easily seen, El País's perspective on daily life in Cuba is called into question by the available evidence. The assertion that the Cuban leaders refuse to recognize their responsibilities vis-à-vis the economic challenges facing the nation does not hold up under scrutiny. Indeed, the country's highest-ranking officials, starting with Raúl Castro, have publicly acknowledged the limitations of the current system and the need for an update of the Cuban economic and social model.

3

A Social Failure?

EVEN MORE SURPRISINGLY, *El País* has invoked the "social failure" of the Cuban Revolution, thereby taking a view that contradicts the opinions expressed by numerous international organizations, all of which recognize that, despite the difficulties and daily vicissitudes, Cuba has reached a level of social justice unparalleled to this day. According to the newspaper, "The Castro system does not have the capacity to provide employment for Cubans or even to feed them."[45] Again, it is necessary to confront the assumptions of the Spanish paper with fact-based reality.

EDUCATION AND HEALTH

In terms of education, the illiteracy rate in Latin America is 11.7 percent and 0.2 percent in Cuba. Enrollment rates in primary level education (up to 11 years) are 92 percent for Latin America and 100 percent for the Caribbean island. The secondary level enrollment rate in education (up to age 14) is 52 percent for Latin America and 99.7 percent for Cuba. Nearly 76 percent of all Latin American children attain middle-school level whereas the figure is 100 percent for Cuban pupils.[46] The Economic and Social Council of the European Union recognizes that "these figures are exceptional among developing countries."[47]

The UNESCO's Department of Education reports that Cuba has the lowest rate of illiteracy and the highest enrollment rates in Latin America, and that Cuban students have attained a knowledge level twice that of other Latin American children. UNESCO also states that "Cuba, although it is one of the poorest countries in Latin America, has the best results in terms of basic education." Juan Cassassus of UNESCO's Latin American Laboratory for the Assessment of the Quality of Education (LLECE) notes that "education has been a top priority in Cuba for forty years. It is truly an education-based society."

His report on education in thirteen Latin American countries shows Cuba leading in all matters of education.[48] Another 2008 study also confirms that Cuba has achieved the best results on the continent in this area."[49]

In its latest report on education, UNESCO emphasizes once again the exceptional results Cuba has achieved:

> In Latin America, learning assessments have highlighted wide differences between countries and deep inequalities within them. Regional surveys of mathematics achievement in primary schools demonstrate both sets of disparities. In 2006, one-third of grade three students in Chile were assessed at level 3 or 4, compared with just 13% in El Salvador. In several countries, high levels of inequality go hand in hand with concentrations of low performance. About 10% of third graders in Argentina performed below level 1 on the mathematics performance scale, while a similar proportion performed at the highest level [UNESCO-OREALC, 2008]. Over half of grade 3 students in Cuba performed at level 4—more than three times that of their peers in Argentina or Chile, for example. Cuba registered by far the highest proportion of students scoring at the highest benchmark and by far the smallest proportion scoring at level 1 or below.[50]

El País published an article about the 2012 report that discusses the situation in Spain, a country that ranks third from the bottom in the European Union in terms of academic failure. Then the paper discusses the situation in Latin America: "The global picture in Latin America is not really better. In light of the advances in universal education, something that was a reality until four years ago, since 2008 many countries are now 'lagging behind.' Few are 'on track,' UNESCO laments."[51]

The Spanish daily, of course, might have mentioned the Cuban exception in Latin America, something the UN agency did not fail to do in its report, but this was not to be. UNESCO stressed that Cuba occupies sixteenth place worldwide—and first place in the Americas—in UNESCO's Education for All Development Index (IDE), which assesses universal primary education, adult literacy education, gender parity, gender equality, and the quality of education in general. By way of comparison, the United States ranked twenty-fifth.[52]

IDE also reports that Cuba is the nation that spends the highest share of its budget, nearly 13 percent of its GDP, on education.[53] This percentage is 7.3 percent in the United States, 6.7 percent in Sweden, 6.4 percent in Finland, 6.3 percent in France, 6.2 percent in the Netherlands, 6 percent in the United Kingdom and Australia, 5.6 percent in Spain, 5.3 percent in Germany, 5.2 percent in Japan, and 4.9 percent in Italy.[54]

Certain indicators allow us to assess the excellence of the Cuban health care system. For example, the global Latin American infant mortality rate is 32 per thousand, but only 4.6 per thousand for Cuba, the lowest in the hemisphere, from Canada to Argentina.[55] While life expectancy is 70 years for Latin Americans, it is 78 years for Cubans. According to the World Health Organization (WHO), Cuba is one of the countries with the largest number of centenarians in relation to its population.[56] The number of physicians per 100,000 is 160 for Latin America and 590 for Cuba.[57]

The American Association for World Health, whose honorary president is Jimmy Carter, notes that the health system in Cuba is "uniformly considered as the preeminent model for the third world."[58] According to the American Public Health Association, "there is no racial barrier to access to health care" and notes that "the example Cuba offers is that of a country with the political will to provide good health care for all its citizens." Cuba is the nation with the highest number of doctors per capita in the world.[59]

The *New England Journal of Medicine*, the most prestigious medical journal in the world, reports: "The Cuban health care system seems unreal. There are too many doctors. Everybody has a family doctor. Everything is free, totally free. . . . Although Cuba has limited resources, the health care system has solved some problems that ours [the United States] has not been able to address."[60]

This specialized journal adds:

This highly structured, prevention-oriented system has produced positive results. Vaccination rates in Cuba are among the highest in the world. The life expectancy of 78 years is virtually identical to that of the United States. The infant mortality rate in Cuba has fallen from over 80 per 1,000 live births in the 1950s to less than five per 1,000, lower than the U.S. rate. . . .

Without doubt, improving health statistics result primarily from improvements in nutrition and education, something that addresses directly the social determinants of health. The literacy rate is 99 percent, and health education is part of the school curriculum. . . . Cuba now has twice as many doctors per capita as the United States.[61]

The Cuban model of HIV prevention and treatment is considered one of the most successful in the world by specialists from the United Nations Development Program, the School of Medicine at Harvard University, and the Pan American Health Organization (PAHO), all of whom regularly travel to Havana to benefit from Cuban expertise in this field.[62]

According to the Human Development Index (HDI) of the United Nations Development Program in 2011, Cuba over the past decade was the only Latin American and the only third world country to rank among the top ten nations in the world on the Human Development Index for three measures—life expectancy, education, and standard of living.[63]

The Havana government currently hosts more than 76,000 students from poor countries and offers them free high-quality university training, while covering all of their expenses. Nearly 6,000 new foreign students are welcomed each year.[64]

International aid provided by the Cuban government does not come at the expense of its own people. Indeed, Daniel Martinez, Regional Director for the Americas of the International Labor Organization (ILO) called the Cuban social security system a "miracle" given the protection it provides workers. "It's almost a miracle compared to other countries," said Martinez, who was equally impressed by the low unemployment rate in Cuba (1.9 percent). According to the ILO, in Latin America, 11 percent of the population is unemployed and nearly 65 percent have no access to social security. In Latin America, one of the great paradoxes lies in the fact that 25 million children are forced to work and 19.5 million adults are unemployed. Cuba is the only country in the world that allows workers in sectors undergoing restructuring, as in the case of the sugar industry, to attend university while maintaining their full salary.[65]

CHILD PROTECTION

According to the World Health Organization (WHO), Cuba, in terms of care provided to mothers and children, is a model for other developing countries.[66] UNICEF, for example, states that "Cuba is a model in terms of child protection."[67] José Juan Ortiz, UNICEF's representative in Havana, reports that "severe malnutrition does not exist in Cuba [because] there exists the political will" to eliminate it. "Here, there are no children in the streets. In Cuba, children are always a priority and that is why they do not suffer from the shortages that affect millions of other children in Latin America, who must work, who are exploited or who find themselves trapped in prostitution networks."[68] Ortiz shared his experience:

> There are millions of children who are exploited every day, who never go to school, millions of boys and girls who do not have an official identity, who do not exist because they have not been counted in the census. We need to bear this in mind since otherwise we would find ourselves talking about a utopian world that conforms to the pretty pictures bandied about in the mass media. Pictures that show us a world that does not in fact exist.[69]

Furthermore,

> Cuba, for more than 50 years, has been a model of protection and promotion of children's rights. Public policies that ensure the protection of children have been a priority for years. Because of this, the country has achieved something truly unique in the developing world. Among the hundreds of millions of boys and girls who suffer serious violations of their rights, who die daily from absolutely preventable causes, none of these children are Cuban. This is a clear demonstration that this level of achievement is possible if states turn their attention to children and make their rights a priority.
>
> The situation of children is not an economic problem. Cuba clearly demonstrates this despite the international crisis, despite the severe impact economic sanctions have on child development, despite being the only country that suffers these sanctions, despite all of this, it is nonetheless possible to guarantee fully the rights of children and reach increasingly higher levels of human development. Cuba is an example for the world as a way to proceed if we are to ensure the rights and the full development of children. The Cuban people have a treasure, the importance of which they themselves do not always

recognize. Cuban children and adolescents are privileged in comparison with the rest of the world.[70]

And finally:

Twenty thousand children die in the world each day, and the overwhelming majority of these deaths are preventable. It is criminal to let children die while we have the means to save them. Were children's issues a global priority, the problems they are victims of would have been resolved a long time ago, as they have been in Cuba. Cuba has always been an example in the area of social development with levels of achievement equal to those of the more developed countries. . . . Cuba knew to teach sharing, solidarity. . . .

The work done in Cuba with juvenile offenders—another great theme and challenge for Latin America and the Caribbean—is exemplary. Here, there are no prison bars for children, rather the system privileges rehabilitation for misguided youth. . . . Further, all children with disabilities receive aid and support, even in their homes if they are not able to get about. This is an exceptional achievement. . . . It is the only country I know where you can celebrate by dancing on International Children's Day.[71]

The UN representative also said: "Because of my work in most other countries, I spend my time burying children. However, in Cuba I spend my time playing with them." He did not hesitate to call the island of Cuba a "paradise of childhood in Latin America."[72]

Similarly, UNICEF reiterates in its 2011 report that Cuba is the only Latin American country—indeed the only third world country—to have eradicated infantile malnutrition.[73] The Spanish daily *El País* has in the past published an article on UNICEF reports in which it pointed out that 146 million children are malnourished and stressed that the two countries in Latin America to have reduced their rates of child malnutrition are Mexico and Brazil.

However, at no point does the article mention the exceptional case of Cuba in this arena.[74]

The non-governmental organization Save the Children, in its *State of the World's Mothers* report, places Cuba at the forefront of developing countries in terms of services offered to mothers, ranking it ahead of Argentina, Israel, and South Korea. In this study, several criteria were taken into account, namely the health care system, the educational level required of trained personnel present during delivery, the dissemination of contraceptive methods, the educational level of women and children, the degree of political and economic equality between men and women, and the level of participation by women in politics and pay equity.[75]

THE BIOTECHNOLOGY SECTOR

Cuba has a cutting-edge biotechnology industry. Its research and drug-manufacturing centers have allowed it to develop dozens of vaccines whose efficacy is recognized by the World Health Organization. Notable examples include those used to prevent meningitis B, leptospirosis, cholera, tosferine, diabetes, hepatitis B, and others used to prevent various forms of cancer. These vaccines are exported to more than twenty-five countries.[76]

Moreover, the world's first vaccine against lung cancer, the Cimavax-EGF, was developed by Cuban scientists at the Molecular Immunology Center in Havana. According to the World Health Organization, this plague causes five million deaths per year mainly because of the worldwide popularity of tobacco. Through the generation of antibodies, this vaccine provides, among other things, the conversion of an advanced-stage cancer into a controllable, chronic disease.[77] In January 2013, Cuba patented yet another new vaccine to be used against cancer, called Racotumomab, which has demonstrated its efficacy in 86 countries.[78]

The American biologist Peter Agre, a Nobel Laureate in chemistry, has praised the Cuban public health system. According to him,

Cuba "is an example for the Western world, which has much to learn for solving problems that persist in other areas of our planet."[79]

The *New England Journal of Medicine* notes that "Cuba has developed its own pharmaceutical industry and now not only manufactures most of the medicines in its basic pharmacopeia, but also fuels an export industry. Resources have been invested in developing biotechnology expertise in order to make Cuba competitive with developed countries."[80]

For its part, UNESCO has welcomed Cuba's scientific advances in the field of biotechnology. Irina Bokova, Director-General of UNESCO since 2009, stated that she was "very impressed" by the level of development reached by the island.[81]

CUBAN HUMANITARIAN INTERNATIONALISM

Since 1963, when its first humanitarian medical mission was sent to Algeria, Cuba has been committed to caring for poor people across the planet, this in the name of international solidarity and the seven principles of Cuban medicine: equality, free, solidarity, accessibility, universality, shared responsibility, and justice.[82] Since then, Cuban humanitarian missions have spread over four continents. They are unique. Indeed, no other nation in the world, including the most developed, has constructed a comparable network of humanitarian cooperation across the planet. Thus, since the launch of this humanitarian project, nearly 132,000 Cuban doctors and other health personnel have volunteered to work in 102 countries.[83] All in all, more than 85 million people around the world have been treated by Cuban doctors, who have saved some 615,000 lives.[84] Currently, 38,868 medical employees, of whom 15,407 are doctors, offer their services in 66 nations.[85]

In 2012, Cuba trained more than 11,000 new doctors, who completed their six-year curriculum in medical schools recognized for the excellence of their teaching. It is the largest medical graduating class in the history of a country that has made the development of medicine and social welfare national priorities. Of these new doctors, 5,315 are Cuban, and 5,694 come from 59 different countries in Latin America, Africa, Asia, and even the United States. A majority are Bolivian (2,400), Peruvian (453), Nicaraguan (429), Ecuadorian (308), Colombian (175), and Guatemalan (170). Thus, in one year, Cuba trained nearly twice the total number of doctors as there were in the entire country before the Revolution in 1959.[86]

When the Revolution triumphed, Cuba had only 6,286 doctors. Of these, 3,000 chose to leave the country for the United States, attracted by the job opportunities that Washington was offering. Within the context of the political and ideological war it was waging against the new government of Fidel Castro, the Eisenhower administration decided to drain the nation of its human capital. This was effective, but it created a serious health crisis.[87]

In response, Cuba pledged to invest heavily in medicine, universalize access to higher education, and introduce a no-cost policy in all courses of study. There are now 24 medical schools (compared to one in 1959) in thirteen of the fifteen Cuban provinces, and the country has more than 43,000 professors of medicine. Since 1959, nearly 109,000 physicians have been trained in Cuba.[88] With a doctor for every 148 inhabitants (67.2 doctors per 10,000 inhabitants; 78,622 in total) according to the World Health Organization, Cuba is the world's best provided nation in this area. The country has 161 hospitals and 452 clinics.[89]

For the 2011–12 school year, the total number of graduates in medical sciences, both Cuban and foreign, representing 21 professional specialties—doctors, stomatologists, nurses, psychologists, health technologists, etc.—rose to 32,171.[90]

HAVANA'S LATIN AMERICAN SCHOOL OF MEDICINE

In addition to the courses offered in the country's 24 medical schools, Cuba also trains foreign students at the Latin American

School of Medicine (ELAM) in Havana. In 1998, after Hurricane Mitch ravaged much of Central America and the Caribbean, Fidel Castro decided to create the Latin American School of Medicine. Opened on November 15, 1999, ELAM's purpose is to train future physicians from third world countries in Cuba.

"Training doctors who are willing to go where they are needed the most and stay as long as necessary has been the goal of our school since its inception," says Dr. Miladys Castilla, deputy rector of ELAM.[91] Currently, 24,000 students from 116 countries of Latin America, the Caribbean, Africa, Asia, Oceania, and even the United States (500 students per class) receive a free education in Cuba. Between the first class of 2005 and that of 2010, some 8,594 young doctors from 54 countries were trained at ELAM.[92] The 2011 and 2012 school years were exceptional with nearly 8,000 graduates receiving their diplomas. In total, nearly 15,000 doctors have been trained at ELAM in 25 specialties.[93]

The World Health Organization has praised the work of ELAM:

> The Latin American School of Medicine in Havana hosts passionate young people from developing countries and sends them home once they become doctors. This is done to promote equity in health services. . . .
>
> ELAM . . . shares our requirement of "social responsibility." The World Health Organization defines the social responsibility of medical schools as "an obligation to ensure that their teaching, research and service activities are designed to meet the priority health concerns of the community, region and/or country they are mandated to serve."
>
> The purpose of ELAM is to train doctors who will ensure public service in poor urban and rural communities by teaching them expanded primary health care skills and the promotion of treatment and rehabilitation. In exchange for a non-binding commitment to practice in underserved areas, students receive a full scholarship along with a small monthly stipend and have no debt upon graduation.

[In terms of recruitment], preference is given to financially disadvantaged applicants who otherwise could not afford to study medicine. "The result is that 75 percent of the students come from communities that need doctors, something that ensures that ethnic minorities as well as indigenous peoples, are well represented. . . ."

The new doctors work in most countries of the Americas, including the United States, as well as in various African countries and many English-speaking countries of the Caribbean region.

At the same time schools like ELAM challenge medical educators in the rest of the world to take social concerns more into consideration. As highlighted by Charles Boelen, former coordinator of the WHO program, Human Resources for Health, "The concept of social responsibility has to be taken into account throughout the world, even in traditional medical circles. . . . The world is in urgent need of those who are dedicated to constructing new paradigms of medical education."[94]

Cuban international aid extends to ten countries in Latin America and to numerous underdeveloped regions of the planet. According to the United Nations Development Program (UNDP), "One of the most successful examples of Cuban cooperation with the third world has been the Integrated Health Program for Central America, the Caribbean, and Africa." In October 1998, when Hurricane Mitch devastated Central America and the Caribbean, the region's heads of state launched a call for international solidarity. According to the UNDP, Cuba was the first to respond positively by canceling Nicaragua's $50 million debt and offering the services of its health personnel.[95]

The Integrated Health Program was then developed and extended to the continents of Africa and Asia. The UNDP points to improvements in all health indicators, including a significant decline in infant mortality in areas where the program has been applied. It is currently in force on three continents and is based on three basic principles:

1. The deployment without charge of health staff for a period of two years, after which a new team replaces them.
2. Training of medical staff at the Latin American School of Medicine in Havana, or at universities created on site under the direction of Cuban teachers.
3. The presence of medical brigades whose members provide their services in rural and medically deprived areas, thereby ensuring that their work does not interfere with that of the local physicians.[96]

Thanks to the election of Hugo Chávez in 1998 and the special relationship the country has established with Cuba, the first recipient to benefit from Cuban human capital was Venezuela. The program of universal access to education, in force since 1998, has achieved exceptional results. With the implementation of a literacy campaign called Robinson I, nearly 1.5 million Venezuelans have been taught to read, write, and count. In December 2005, UNESCO declared that Venezuela had eradicated illiteracy. Robinson II was implemented to bring the total population up to secondary level. In addition, there are the Ribas and Sucre missions that have allowed tens of thousands of young adults to undertake university studies. In 2010, 97 percent of all Venezuelan children were attending school.[97]

In terms of health, the national public system was created to ensure free access to health care for all Venezuelans. Barrio Adentro I has conducted some 300 million patient consultations in the 4,469 medical centers that have been established since 1998. In all, nearly 17 million people have been treated. In 1998, fewer than three million people had regular access to health care. With the new services it has been possible to save over 104,000 lives.

The infant mortality rate has been reduced to less than 10 in 1,000.[98] Venezuela has moved from 83rd in 2000 (0.656) to 73rd in 2011 (0.735) in the classification rankings of the Human Development Index (HDI) of the United Nations Program for Development, and has been moved up to the HDI's developed nations category.[99] Similarly, according to the UNDP, Venezuela, which has the lowest Gini coefficient in Latin America, is the least unequal country in the region.[100] Economist Luis Alberto Matos, an energy expert, has spoken of the "landmark cooperation" between Cuba and Venezuela: "Who can deny the immense contributions this country has made to Venezuela in improving the areas of health, agriculture, and sport, not to mention culture?[101]

Through ALBA (Bolivarian Alliance for the Peoples of Our America) and the social programs launched by the government of Evo Morales between 2006 and July 2011, the Cuban Medical Brigade in Bolivia has conducted 48 million patient consultations and in so doing has saved 49,821 lives.[102] Bolivia has been able to improve its health indicators with a decrease in infant mortality from 58 per 1,000 in 2007 to 51 per 1,000 in 2009,[103] a reduction of nearly 14 percent in three years. Between 2006 and 2009, nearly 545 health centers were established throughout the country. In terms of education, Bolivia, with the elimination of illiteracy in 824,000 people, was declared by UNESCO to be illiteracy-free territory on December 20, 2008.

The *Yo Sí Puedo Seguir* (Yes I Can Continue) program, designed to enable people to attain middle school level, has benefited some 52,000 people. Nearly 1,540 schools have been built. In terms of higher education, three indigenous universities have been created. Extreme poverty has been reduced by 6 percent, from 37.8 percent to 31.8 percent.[104] Bolivia has improved its HDI of 0.649 in 2005 to 0.663 in 2011, while maintaining its ranking of 108th in the HDI list of countries worldwide.[105]

In Nicaragua, the *Yo Sí Puedo* (Yes I Can) program allowed UNESCO in 2009 to declare the country free of illiteracy. Through ALBA, Nicaragua has also been able to solve its severe energy crisis, something that had been responsible for power cuts of 16 hours a day.[106] Several fully equipped hospitals have been built throughout the country offering free health care to the entire population. They work in part thanks to the presence of Cuban medical personnel. The HDI ranking rose from 0.582 in 2009 to 0.589 in 2011, placing Nicaragua 129th worldwide.[107]

In Ecuador, the coming to power in 2006 of Rafael Correa led to an unprecedented social revolution. The health budget rose from $437 million in 2006 to $3.43 billion in 2010. The education budget has increased from $235 million in 2006 to $940.7 billion in 2010. The level of education through the secondary level, for the poorest quintile of the population, increased from 30 percent to 40 percent between 2006 and 2010. The household shopping basket level increased from 68 percent to 89 percent. At the national level, poverty fell by 7 percent over the same period and by 13 percent for Afro-Ecuadorians, thereby pulling out of poverty some 700,000 of the five million needy persons that the nation counted in 2006.[108] Thus the HDI rose from 0.716 in 2009 to 0.720 in 2011, ranking the country 83rd.[109] Ecuador plans to completely eradicate child malnutrition in 2015, thereby joining Cuba, currently the only Latin American and third world country to rid itself of this scourge, according to UNICEF.[110]

On September 19, 2005, following the tragedy caused by Hurricane Katrina in New Orleans, Cuba created the Henry Reeve Brigade,[111] a medical contingent of 10,000 health professionals specializing in natural disasters. Havana, at the time, offered to send 1,586 doctors to the United States to help the victims of hurricane Katrina, an offer that was refused by then-president George W. Bush.[112]

The Henry Reeve Brigade has intervened notably on several continents. For example, following the earthquake that devastated Pakistan in November 2005, some 2,564 doctors arrived on site and treated victims for more than eight months. Thirty-two field hospitals were constructed and then offered to local health authorities. More than 1.8 million patients were treated and 2,086 lives were saved. No other nation in the world offered equivalent help. Even the United States, Islamabad's principal ally, established only two field hospitals and sent a medical team that stayed for no more than eight weeks.[113] The British newspaper the *Independent* pointed out that the Cuban medical brigade was the first to arrive on the scene and the last to leave the country.[114]

Earlier, after the tsunami that devastated the Pacific region in 2004, Cuba dispatched several humanitarian missions to provide assistance to victims, often abandoned by local authorities. Many rural areas of Kiribati, Sri Lanka, and East Timor are still dependent on Cuban medical assistance.[115] A medical school was even established in East Timor, dedicated to training young students from that country. The Solomon Islands and Papua New Guinea requested that Havana provide them with similar support and have since signed cooperative agreements.[116]

After the May 2006 earthquake in Java, Indonesia, Cuba sent several medical missions. Ronny Rockito, Indonesian Regional Health Coordinator, praised the work of the 135 Cuban professionals who set up two field hospitals. According to him, the work carried out by the Cubans had a greater impact than that of any other country. "I appreciate the Cuban medical teams. Their style is very friendly and the level of care they provide is excellent. Everything is free and there has been no support from my government for any of this. We thank Fidel Castro. Many villagers begged the Cuban doctors to stay."[117]

The most recent, as well as the most emblematic, case of Cuban medical cooperation concerns Haiti. The January 2010 magnitude 7 earthquake caused dramatic human and property damage.[118] According to the Haitian authorities, the heavy balance sheet included at least 230,000 dead, 300,000 injured, and 1.2 million homeless.[119] The Cuban medical brigade, on site since 1998, was the first to bring aid to the country and treated nearly 40 percent of the victims.[120]

In October 2010, Nepalese UN troops inadvertently introduced the cholera virus into Haiti. According to the UN, the epidemic was discovered by the Cuban medical team of Dr. Jorge Luis Quiñones. It killed 6,600 people and sickened some 476,000 others, a figure that represents nearly 5 percent of the total population of 10 million. The UN has called this the world's highest rate of cholera. The *New York Times*, in an article on the key role played by Cuban doctors, notes: "The Cuban medical mission played an important role in the detection of the epidemic and presses on in Haiti, winning accolades from donors and diplomats for staying on the front lines and undertaking a broader effort to remake this country's shattered health care system."[121]

For his part, UN Special Envoy Paul Farmer observed that in December 2010, when the epidemic was at its peak with an unprecedented mortality rate and the world watching, "half of the NGOs had already left, while the Cubans were still present." According to the Haitian Ministry of Health, Cuban doctors have saved more than 76,000 people in 67 medical units under their responsibility, with only 272 deaths, that is to say, a mortality rate of 0.36 percent, compared to a rate of 1.4 percent in the rest of the country. Since December 2010, no deaths have occurred among patients treated by the Cuban physicians.[122]

El País reported extensively on the earthquake in Haiti.[123] At no time, however, has it mentioned Cuba's humanitarian aid, which has been not only the most important for Haiti, but also the most long-lasting. Worse, in an article that appeared in its edition of January 15, 2010, the paper included a list of 23 countries that have provided financial, material or medical aid to the population. No mention of Cuba was made.[124]

In addition to dispatching medical personnel around the world, Cuba's training of doctors from third world countries must be taken into account. Since 1959, thousands of foreign doctors have been trained in Cuba and nine medical schools run by Cuban teachers have been constructed, primarily in Africa.[125]

According to the UNDP, Cuban humanitarian aid represents, proportionately, a higher share of the average GDP than that of the 18 most highly developed nations. The UNDP reported:

> The cooperation offered by Cuba inscribes itself in a South-South context of cooperation. It is not done for profit, but is

instead offered as an expression of the principle of solidarity and, to the extent possible, of shared costs. Nonetheless, over the years Cuba has provided grant assistance to the poorest countries, and has been very flexible about the form or structure of the collaboration. . . . In almost all cases, Cuban aid was provided free of charge, although beginning in 1977, with some high-income countries, mainly oil-producing states, a form of compensated cooperation was developed. The high levels of development achieved by Cuba in the areas of health, education, and sport have led to cooperation primarily in these areas, although there has been cooperation in other sectors, such as construction, fishing, and agriculture."[126]

OPERATION MIRACLE

According to the World Health Organization, there are currently almost 285 million people who are visually impaired worldwide, 39 million of them blind and 246 million who have experienced a decrease in visual acuity. Almost 90 percent of them live in the third world. The main causes of visual impairment are uncorrected refractive errors such as myopia, hyperopia, or astigmatism (43 percent), cataracts (33 percent), and glaucoma (2 percent). The organization points out that nearly 80 percent of all visual impairments are treatable and adds that "cataracts remain the leading cause of blindness." These eye diseases affect primarily 65 percent of those over the age of fifty (20 percent of the world's population), a percentage that increases with the aging of the population. At the same time, 19 million children are also affected.[127]

Faced with this situation, and again within the context of the ALBA, Cuba and Venezuela agreed in 2004 to launch an extensive continental humanitarian campaign named Operación Milagro (Operation Miracle). The program is designed to offer free operations that normally cost between $5,000 and $10,000, depending upon the country, to poor Latin Americans with cataracts and other eye diseases. This humanitarian mission has since been extended to other latitudes (Africa and Asia). Operación Milagro includes the participation of 165 Cuban institutions. It has 49 eye centers in fourteen countries in Latin America and the Caribbean (Cuba, Venezuela, Bolivia, Ecuador, Haiti, Honduras, Panama, Guatemala, St. Vincent and the Grenadines, Guyana, Paraguay, Grenada, Nicaragua, and Uruguay).[128]

By the first of January 2008, a million people had undergone operations.[129] In 2011, more than two million people from 35 countries had recovered their sight.[130] Within the framework of the ALBA accords, the Venezuelan population was the first to benefit, with more than 178,000 operations to date. Bolivia has also benefited greatly from Cuban medical cooperation, with 600,105 operations.[131] Bolivian president Evo Morales welcomed the presence of Cuban doctors and the integrative and supportive role of ALBA.[132]

Other countries have also benefited from the humanitarian internationalism of Operación Milagro. Thus 100,000 Ecuadorians,[133] 61,000 Nicaraguans,[134] 61,000 Jamaicans,[135] 50,000 Panamanians,[136] 48,255 Brazilians, 35,245 Argentines, 22,280 Peruvians, and 312 Paraguayans, among others, have had their sight restored.[137] U.S. citizens from the most disadvantaged groups have also benefited from Operation Miracle.[138]

The most emblematic case is undoubtedly that of Mario Terán, a retired Bolivian army sergeant who killed Ernesto Che Guevara on October 9, 1967, in a little school in La Higuera, Bolivia. He was living in anonymity in Santa Cruz, Bolivia. He subsisted on his small pension as a former soldier but had lost his sight, the victim of a cataract he could not afford to have treated.[139] Through Operación Milagro, Terán recovered from his disability. Pablo Ortiz, a Bolivian journalist who works for the daily *El Deber* of Santa Cruz, reported the story: "Terán had cataract problems and, thanks to Operación Milagro, was operated on by Cuban doctors, an operation that was totally free of cost." He then provided more details: "The guy was totally unknown. No one had any idea who he was and he was completely destitute when he went to the

Operación Milagro hospital. Nobody recognized him for who he was and he was accepted for an operation. It is his own son who told us all this, and who came to our newspaper in hopes of expressing his appreciation publicly."[140]

In 2009, on the occasion of the 10,000th surgical procedure performed in the José Martí Eye Center, Operación Milagro was awarded the Citizenship Award for Excellence by the Uruguayan Latin American Development Center (CELADE), sponsored, among others, by the Organization of American States (OAS) because of its solidarity and humane values.[141]

The Canadian press even reported that a number of subjects of the British Crown, for lack of financial resources, prefer to seek care and be operated on in Cuba, a country known for its excellent care and prices that are affordable for Westerners.[142]

AID TO AFRICA

In 2006, the World Health Organization launched an emergency appeal to the international community to come to the aid of Africa. Meningitis A and C had struck 23 African countries located in the so-called Meningitis Belt that stretches from Senegal to Ethiopia. These diseases affected nearly 100,000 people and caused more than 5,000 deaths each year. In the struggle against them, the UN agency had a compelling need for polysaccharides vaccines. To treat the 430 million people in the region, it would be necessary to massively produce this preventive agent.[143]

At the time, Sanofi, the French company that manufactured these vaccines, had significantly reduced production because of the low profit margin, thereby creating a health emergency. WHO then called upon all laboratories, both public and private, to begin production of this type of vaccine. Only two third world public laboratories responded to this appeal: the Carlos Finlay Institute of Cuba and Brazil's Bio-Manguinhos Institute. All of the multinational pharmaceutical companies turned a deaf ear to the request.[144]

These two entities joined together and created the vax-MEN-AC vaccine at a price of 95 cents a dose; in other words it was produced at a price one-twentieth of that produced by Sanofi. A total of 19 million doses were produced and distributed in Africa by WHO, UNICEF, Doctors Without Borders, and the International Red Cross, saving tens of thousands of lives.[145] The prestigious U.S. journal *Science* welcomed this example of "South-South cooperation" and appealed for the extension of this model to the rest of the world.[146]

El País did not fail to publicize a humanitarian action funded by the foundation of billionaire Bill Gates, in which 10,000 doses of tuberculosis vaccine were distributed. Indeed, it devoted a long article to lauding him.[147] On the other hand, the Madrid newspaper did not see fit to devote a single line to the action of Cuba and Brazil, two Latin American nations that, when faced with the indifference of the developed nations toward this African drama, distributed nearly 20 million doses.

THE *YO SÍ PUEDO* PROGRAM

UNESCO reports that there are 796 million illiterate adults in the world, a figure that equals 17 percent of the world's total population. Over 98 percent are in third world countries and nearly two-thirds are women. Seventy-three percent of the population of Sub-Saharan Africa and South and West Asia is illiterate. In absolute terms, the number of illiterate people in these regions continues to grow. In terms of children, only 44 percent are enrolled in pre-primary centers (148 million), which means that 56 percent do not have access to this level of education (222 million). At the primary level, 67 million children do not attend school. UNESCO has launched an appeal to reduce illiteracy by 50 percent by 2015. The UN agency noted that progress in this area "has been disappointing at best and sporadic at worst." In order "to reverse this trend, necessity requires that the governments of the world act with determination."[148] However, UNESCO noted one exception: Latin America and the Caribbean. This exception is due in part to the *Yo Sí Puedo* program:

> The *Yo Sí Puedo* [Yes I Can] program introduced in 2003 by the Cuban Government . . . has been met with a very positive response. Operational since 2008 in 12 of the 19 Latin American countries, it is part of a wider strategy for achieving universal literacy in the Plurinational State of Bolivia, Ecuador, Nicaragua, Panama and the Bolivarian Republic of Venezuela.[149]

Based on the philosophy of José Martí, which can be summarized in this brief quote, "Every human being has the right to education, but in exchange must contribute to the education of others," the Latin American and Caribbean Pedagogical Institute of Cuba launched, in 2003, *Yo Sí Puedo*, a program designed to teach adults to read and write. The acquisition of reading, writing, and arithmetic skills is essential to meaningful participation in citizenship. It constitutes the first line of defense against exclusion and poverty, and leads to the realization of what José Martí called "full human dignity." UNESCO notes that "education saves lives: the higher the academic achievement level of the mother, the more the infant mortality rate declines." Thus, if all women were educated through the high school level, 1.8 million children would be saved each year. Another consequence is that children's health would be better protected: "It is less likely that children whose mothers have studied will be stunted or underweight."[150]

Because of the territorial dispersion of illiterate populations, *Yo Sí Puedo* is implemented by means of radio and television. Through the use of communications technology, distance education has proven to be effective. This method, developed by the finest Cuban specialists under the direction of master teacher Leonela Inés Relys Díaz, makes it possible to reach a large number of people and ensures the efficient and economic use of human and material capital as well as financial resources. Furthermore, it does not require a brick-and-mortar educational institution for its implementation. Based on constant stimulation and a simple process—moving from numbers to letters—and listening/reading and listening/writing sequences, it is divided into three stages (basic learning, teaching reading, and writing and consolidation) that allow the growth of individual work as well as improving the self-esteem of the student. It also encourages family cooperation and creates linkages between literacy students and the illiterate. The possibility of using the method at home avoids the psychological effects that others may have on personal learning and increases one's motivation to become literate. The method is based on the fundamental principle of voluntarism, which tends to increase its efficiency.[151]

A full diagnosis intended to assess socioeconomic, geographical, political, cultural, and religious literacy in a given region is performed. Implementation also requires an assessment of the number of radios and televisions present in a particular region. Another study assesses results obtained in previous literacy efforts. An in-depth knowledge of the characteristics of the illiterate population is considered to be a prerequisite to the development of radio and television courses.

Several frameworks are established to allow control of the literacy process and to ensure the best results. The work is both individual and collective at the same time, with a regular visit from the professor to his students. In each course, topics of interest such as health, family, the elderly, the environment, history, and culture are discussed. Learners receive four to five 30-minute lessons per week by television for a period of three months (32.5 hours or 65 class hours) and a set of seven teaching cards. For radio, the set consists of twenty-five 60-minute tapes representing fifty courses, 32 teaching cards, and a guide for the class monitor.

Yo Sí Puedo has been successfully implemented in Venezuela, where more than a million and a half people are no longer illiterate, and in Bolivia, Ecuador, and Nicaragua, which are, according to UNESCO, the only Latin American nations to have freed themselves of illiteracy in the past decade. It is also used in many other countries on the continent and in other parts of the world such as New Zealand, and is implemented in several languages, including French and certain indigenous languages such as Guaraní and Maori.

The *Yo Sí Puedo* program is also used in developed countries such as Spain and Australia. The city of Seville has engaged the services of Cuban teachers in a project coordinated by Professor Carlos M. Molina Soto that is aimed at teaching reading and writing to its citizens.[152] Upon completion of a study commissioned by the mayor, it was found that some 34,000 of the 700,000 residents of the Andalusian capital were completely illiterate. Within two years, 1,100 adults were rendered literate in thirty literacy centers opened for this purpose. Other municipalities in Spain, which has nearly two million illiterate citizens, are examining the possibility of applying the Cuban method within their territory.[153] This information seems to have escaped the discernment of the Madrid daily newspaper, however.

In Australia, the Cuban literacy program is used with the Aboriginal population—some 60 percent are functionally illiterate—who learn to read and write in three months. In addition to reading, writing, and basic algebra, the program offers them the opportunity to learn to use new technologies. The Cuban program is supported by the Australian government, the University of New England, and the Aboriginal Land Council.[154] It is to be noted that, according to the United Nations, Australia ranks second in the world in terms of human development, just behind Norway.[155]

Yo Sí Puedo was awarded UNESCO's King Sejong Literacy Prize in 2006 for its contribution to the education of humanity. Irina Bokova, Director-General of the UN agency, welcomed the method, highlighting it as an exemplar of South-South cooperation.[156] Since 2003, more than seven million people from 28 different countries have learned to read, write, and count thanks to the program.[157] Miguel Livina, the representative of UNESCO's

Regional Office for Culture in Latin America and the Caribbean, said the Cuban method should be considered seriously by other governments and international institutions. This method was also publicly recognized in 2010 at the XX Ibero-American Summit.[158]

A new program called *Yo, Sí Puedo Seguir* (Yes, I can carry on), designed to improve the knowledge level of literate people, has also been launched in nations where *Yo Sí Puedo* had been implemented successfully.

THE CHILDREN OF CHERNOBYL

Cuba's role in treating the victims of the nuclear disaster that occurred on April 26, 1986, at Chernobyl in Ukraine, a tragedy that killed 40,000 people and contaminated millions, remains unknown to this day.[159] Since the inception in 1990 of the Tarará Humanitarian Program, developed as a response to the worst nuclear accident in history, nearly 30,000 children aged five to fifteen were treated without cost in Cuba.[160]

The British newspaper the *Guardian* reported:

> Despite its isolation and economic stagnation, Cuba continued to care for these children. The difference between the Tarará program and others—such as the exchange of Cuban medical expertise for Venezuelan oil—is that there is no economic gain. The program even survived the Cuban economic crisis of the early 90s, the so-called "special period," that occurred after the fall of the Soviet bloc. . . . Dr. Julio Medina, general coordinator of the program, recently told the Cuban newspaper *Granma*: "It's simple: we do not give what we have in excess, we share all that we have.[161]

The children are cared for at the Tarará hospital, some 20 kilometers east of Havana, in a region that enjoys an exceptional microclimate favorable to healing. Most suffer from cancers, including skin, thyroid, leukemia, alopecia, and vitiligo as well as birth defects. Furthermore, thanks to this program, Cuba has created a database on nuclear contamination that is unique in the world and in turn has allowed Cuban scientists and researchers to develop techniques to study the effects of nuclear contamination on human DNA.[162]

"For many mothers, Cuba was their only hope," says Svetlana Zaslavskaya, whose child was treated on the island.[163] Nikola Efimovich Polischuk, Ukrainian Minister of Health, said that no nation in the world had done so much for child victims of the Chernobyl nuclear disaster as Cuba.[164] "In difficult times for the people of Ukraine, Cuba was one of the first countries to reach out to the health of children affected," he added.[165] For his part, Konstantin Grishenko, Ukrainian Minister of Foreign Affairs, expressed gratitude to the government in Havana: "We will never forget what Cuba has done for us."[166]

CRIME PREVENTION

In terms of security, Cuba is also an exemplar. As Elias Carranza, director of the Latin American Institute of the United Nations for the Prevention of Crime and the Treatment of Offenders, said, Cuba has eradicated social exclusion through "progress made in reducing crime." This is the "safest country in the region [and] the situation with regard to crime and insecurity across the continent has deteriorated during the past three decades with the increasing number of deaths both within and outside of prisons."[167]

CIVIL DEFENSE

The Cuban Civil Defense System, created at the time of the triumph of the Revolution to deal with natural disasters, is an example for the entire continent. Regularly subject to hurricanes and other weather events, the island of Cuba, like the entire Caribbean region, each year must face the fury of nature. Unlike neighboring countries, including the United States, where casualties are often significant, the government of Havana has been able to minimize the number of deaths.[168]

This national system commands all of the resources of the country in the case of natural disaster. The work is first and foremost preventive and includes the evacuation of people living in high-risk areas. These evacuations can move up to a million people in a period of a few days.

All of the country's resources are made available to the displaced residents, including schools, businesses, theaters, libraries, gyms, and even the Capitolio, the old Cuban Parliament building. All are transformed into temporary dormitories for the duration of the hurricane season, with food service and a continuous medical presence.[169]

The Cuban Civil Defense System is structured around zones of defense made up of citizens who are not involved in rescue operations, but who are responsible for monitoring the condition of buildings and identifying those that could collapse if a hurricane were to strike. After the hurricane has passed, a "recovery phase" is enacted, and human and material resources are sent to the affected areas.[170]

Cuba has also implemented a system of disaster medicine. In this regard, the Center for International Policy in Washington, led by Wayne S. Smith, former U.S. ambassador to Cuba, reports that "the effectiveness of the Cuban system is not in doubt. Only a few Cubans have lost their lives in the 16 largest hurricanes to hit the island in the last decade. The likelihood of being killed by a hurricane in the United States is 15 times greater than in Cuba."[171]

The report adds:

> In contrast to the United States, disaster medicine in Cuba is an integral part of the medical curriculum and educating the population on how to respond to disasters begins in primary

school. . . . Even small children take part in drills, learning first aid and survival techniques, often through cartoons, as well as how to grow medicinal herbs and to find food, should disaster strike. The result is an ingrained culture of prevention and preparation second to none.[172]

THE DEVELOPMENT OF URBAN AGRICULTURE

The United Nations Food and Agriculture Organization (FAO) has praised the development of urban agriculture in Cuba. Marcio Porto, FAO's Cuban representative, assures us that the Caribbean island is a model for other Latin American countries to follow. The production of food within densely populated areas is highly beneficial for the economy because it provides substantial advantages in the face of high oil prices.[173]

The UN report *The State of Food Insecurity in the World 2012* shows that the only countries that have eradicated hunger in Latin America are Cuba, Chile, Venezuela, and Uruguay. On the Latin American continent, 49 million people suffer from hunger, not because of food production, which potentially is sufficient to feed the entire population of the Western Hemisphere, but rather because of a lack of financial resources.[174]

According to FAO, "The measures taken by Cuba in the update of its economic model aimed at achieving food sufficiency can become an example for humanity." The agency adds that "with the measures it has taken in the decentralization of land linked to a perspective that aims at providing food sufficiency, the Cuban strategy becomes quite interesting, especially in the areas of nutrition, sovereignty, and autonomy over the food produced." In terms of the twenty-first-century debate over the issues of extreme poverty, undernourishment, and malnutrition, Cuba has already solved these problems: "For some time now, among the 33 countries in the region, undernourishment has been eradicated in Cuba, with impressive results." The FAO cannot say enough about the

Caribbean island: "This is an excellent example of success because Cuba is surrounded by a group of neighboring islands that have not yet been able to achieve what Cuba has already accomplished. In Cuba, despite a hard and unjust blockade, the current strategy has moved to another level: the quality of the food itself."[175]

In a letter to Fidel Castro, José Graziano da Silva, Director-General of FAO, praised the island's outstanding results in the eradication of hunger:

> I have the honor to address you in my capacity as Director-General of the United Nations Food and Agriculture Organization, to sincerely congratulate you and all of the Cuban people for having fulfilled the goal set in advance by the World Food Summit, held in Rome in November 1996, where it was proposed to halve the number of undernourished people in every country before 2015. As you may recall, you honored us with your presence at this summit and delivered a brief but powerful speech, which still lingers in the collective memory of our organization. You concluded by saying: "The bells that toll for those who die of hunger each day, will toll tomorrow for all of humanity if mankind does not wish, does not know how, or somehow fails to be wise enough to save itself." And I am told that during a press conference that followed the summit you said that even if the target were achieved we would not know what to say to the other half of humanity not yet freed from the scourge of hunger. These are concepts that still retain their meaning and their value today.
>
> Seventeen years have passed and I take great satisfaction in informing you that, through a decision taken by its members and for the first time in its history, the FAO Conference, to be held next June in Rome, will adopt the total eradication of hunger as the number one goal of our organization.
>
> I renew my congratulations on your country's important achievement and express my best wishes of well-being and success for you and for all of the Cuban people.[176]

PROTECTING THE ENVIRONMENT

Since the triumph of the Revolution, Cuba has made environmental protection a national priority. Thus, while the phenomenon of deforestation is a reality throughout the rest of the world, Cuba's forest area now represents 24.54 percent of the national territory as opposed to only 14 percent in 1959. Cuba is the only country in the world in which the current forest area is greater than what it was fifty years ago.[177]

Cuban expertise in environmental protection is recognized by many international institutions. In 2006, the Cuban Renewable Energy project of the University of Oriente won the World Energy Globe Award that is given each year to initiatives that foster more efficient and sustainable use of natural resources in the area of energy consumption. This prize is awarded jointly by several global institutions including the UN, the European Renewable Energy Council, and the World Bank, among others.[178]

The World Wildlife Fund (WWF), the largest international organization for the protection of the environment, with more than five million members and a presence in more than 100 countries, stressed in its annual report, *Living Planet*, that Cuba is the only nation in the world to have achieved sustainable development:

> Sustainable development is a commitment to improve the quality of human life while living within the carrying capacity of the ecosystems that sustain us. The Human Development Index is used by the United Nations Development Program as an indicator of well-being and its footprints are measures of the demands we place on the biosphere. The progress of nations toward sustainable development can be measured by crossing the HDI and the footprint. The HDI is calculated on the basis of life expectancy, literacy, education, and GDP per person. The UNDP considers that a country has a high Human Development Index if its HDI value is greater than 0.8. For the footprint, we consider that one that is less than

1.8 global hectares per person, that is to say the average bio-capacity available per person, is indicative of sustainability on a global scale.

Successful sustainable development implies, at the least, that the world as a whole meets both criteria at the same time. . . . Neither the world as a whole, nor any region, taken separately or together meets both criteria of sustainable development. Only Cuba has succeeded, according to the data that countries provide the United Nations.[179]

THE TRIBUTE OF NELSON MANDELA

The fundamental role of Cuba in the liberation of Africa remains unknown to the general public. Algeria was the first African country to benefit from Cuban internationalist aid. In December 1961, the National Liberation Front (FLN), the main Algerian independence movement, received a large quantity of weapons that proved vital in the fight against French colonialism. Fidel Castro, then in open conflict with the United States, had not hesitated to jeopardize the relationship between his country and a great Western power such as that of the France of General De Gaulle in order to rescue the Algerian people. Thereafter, Congo—where Che Guevara fought—Guinea-Bissau, Angola, Namibia, and South Africa, among others, benefited from Cuban solidarity.[180]

One of the most vibrant tributes to Cuba has undoubtedly been that of Nelson Mandela, South African hero in the struggle against apartheid, president of South Africa, and Nobel Peace Prize laureate. Following his release on February 11, 1990, Mandela chose to go to Cuba on July 26, 1991, for his first trip abroad. He explained this choice, one that surprised many observers:

Today, this is revolutionary Cuba, internationalist Cuba, the country that has done so much for the people of Africa. The Cuban people hold a special place in the hearts of the people

of Africa. The Cuban internationalists have made a contribution to the independence, freedom, and justice in Africa,
unparalleled for its principled and selfless character. From its
earliest days, the Cuban Revolution has been a source of inspiration to all freedom-loving peoples. We admire the sacrifice
of the Cuban people in maintaining their independence and
sovereignty in the face of a vicious imperialist-orchestrated
campaign to destroy the impressive achievements of the
Cuban Revolution. . . .

We admire the achievements of the Cuban Revolution in
the sphere of social welfare. We note the transformation from
colonial backwardness to universal literacy. We acknowledge
your advances in the fields of health, education, and science.
There are many things we can learn from your experience. In
particular we are moved by your affirmation of the historical
ties with the African continent and the people of Africa. Your
consistent commitment to the systematic eradication of racism
is unparalleled. But the most important lesson you have for us
is that no matter what the odds, no matter under what difficulties you have had to struggle, there can be no surrender! It is a
case of freedom or death! . . .

We also honor the great Che Guevara, whose revolutionary
exploits, including those on our own continent, were too powerful for any prison censors to hide from us. The life of Che is
an inspiration to all human beings who cherish freedom. We
will always honor his memory!

We come here with a sense of a great debt that is owed to
Cuba. What other country can point to a record of greater self-
lessness than Cuba has displayed in its relations with Africans?
How many countries of the world benefit from Cuban health
workers or educationists? . . . Where is the country that has
sought Cuban help and has had it refused? How many countries under the threat from imperialism or struggling for
national liberation have been able to count on Cuban support?

It was in prison that I first heard of the massive assistance that the Cuban internationalist forces provided to the people of Angola, on such a scale that one hesitated to believe, when the Angolans came under combined attack of South African, CIA-financed FNLA, and Zairian troops in 1975. We in Africa are used to being victims of countries wanting to carve up our territory or subvert our sovereignty. It is unparalleled in history to have another people rise to the defense of one of us. We know also that this was a popular action in Cuba. We are aware that those who fought and died in Angola were only a small proportion of those who volunteered. For the Cuban people internationalism is not merely a word but something that we have seen practiced to the benefit of large sections of humankind. We know that the Cuban forces were willing to withdraw shortly after repelling the 1975 invasion, but the continued aggression from Pretoria made this impossible.

Your presence and the reinforcement of your forces in the Battle of Cuito Cuanavale was of truly historic significance. The crushing defeat of the racist army at Cuito Cuanavale was a victory for the whole of Africa. This overwhelming defeat of the racist army at Cuito Cuanavale provided the possibility for Angola to enjoy peace and consolidate its own sovereignty. The defeat of the racist army allowed the struggling people of Namibia to finally win their independence! The decisive defeat of the apartheid aggressors destroyed the myth of the invincibility of the white oppressors! The defeat of the apartheid army was an inspiration to the struggling people inside South Africa! Without the defeat of Cuito Cuanavale our organizations would not have been unbanned! The defeat of the racist army at Cuito Cuanavale has made it possible for me to be here today! Cuito Cuanavale was a milestone in the history of the struggle for southern African liberation! Cuito Cuanavale has been a turning point in the struggle to free the continent and our country from the scourge of apartheid. . . .

I must say that when we wanted to take up arms we approached numerous Western governments for assistance and we were never able to see any but the most junior ministers. When we visited Cuba we were received by the highest officials and were immediately offered whatever we wanted or needed. This was our earliest experience with Cuban internationalism! The decisive defeat of Cuito Cuanavale altered the balance of forces within the region and substantially reduced the capacity of the Pretoria regime to destabilize its neighbors. This, in combination with our people's struggles within the country was crucial in bringing Pretoria to realize that it would have to talk. . . .

You are with us because both of our organizations, the Communist Party of Cuba and the ANC, are fighting for the oppressed to ensure that those who make the wealth enjoy its fruits. Your great apostle José Martí said, "With the poor people of this earth I want to share my fate." We in the ANC will always stand with the poor and rightless. Not only do we stand with them. We will ensure sooner rather than later that they rule the land of their birth, that in the words of the Freedom Charter, "The people shall govern." And when that moment arrives it will have been made possible not only by our efforts but through the solidarity, support, and encouragement of the great Cuban people![181]

INTERNATIONAL RECOGNITION

All international institutions have praised the Cuban social system, thereby contradicting the assertions of the newspaper *El País*. According to the World Bank:

Cuba has become internationally recognized for its achievements in the areas of education and health, with social service delivery outcomes that surpass most countries in the developing world and in some areas match first-world standards. Since the Cuban Revolution in 1959, and the subsequent establishment of a one-party communist government, the country has created a social service system that guarantees universal access to education and health care provided by the state. This model has enabled Cuba to achieve near universal literacy, the eradication of certain diseases, widespread access to potable water and basic sanitation, and one of the lowest infant mortality rates and longest life expectancies in the region.

A review of Cuba's social indicators reveals a pattern of almost continuous improvement from the 1960s through the end of the 1980s. Several major indices, such as life expectancy and infant mortality, continued to improve during the country's economic crisis of the 1990s. . . . Today, Cuba's social performance is among the best in the developing world, as documented by numerous international sources including the World Health Organization, the United Nations Development Program and other UN agencies, and the World Bank. Cuba outperforms both Latin America and the Caribbean and other middle-income countries in the most important education indicators, health, and public safety.[182]

For its part, the United Nations Population Fund noted that Cuba "adopted more than a half-century ago very advanced social programs that have enabled the country to achieve social and demographic results comparable to those of developed countries." The Fund added that "Cuba demonstrates that the limitations of developing economies are not necessarily insurmountable obstacles to the progress of health, demographic change, and well-being."[183]

All of the information on the Cuban social system, from education to health care, from child protection to the prevention of crime, from the biotechnology sector to humanitarian internationalism, from Operación Milagro to the *Yo Sí Puedo* program, from the Latin American School of Medicine to the development of urban agriculture and environmental protection through Civil Defense—all corroborated by the most prominent international institutions—has, it seems, escaped the *El País* daily. Once again, the assertions of the Iberian newspaper, which describes the Cuban system as a "social failure," run counter to the analyses of the most prominent international institutions.

4

The Issue of Human Rights

IN AN ARTICLE DATED October 28, 2010, *El País*, citing the conflicted relations between Havana and Brussels, reported that "Cuba refuses to normalize relations with the European Union,"[184] a statement that is, at the very least, inaccurate. In fact, since 1996, it has been the Europe of the 27 that has imposed unilaterally a Common Position, something that has become the pillar of Brussels' foreign policy vis-à-vis Havana, and it is this Common Position that constitutes an obstacle to the full normalization of relations with the island. The Common Position states that the resumption of bilateral relations is dependent upon improvements in the situation of human rights in Cuba.[185]

In his article, the journalist Mauricio Vicent fails to highlight four key aspects of the EU policy vis-à-vis Havana: its unilateral character, its discriminatory scope, its contradictory logic, and its illegitimate basis. The only country in the Americas, from Canada to Argentina, to suffer the imposition of such a policy of isolation is Cuba. However, according to Amnesty International, Cuba is far from being the worst performer on the continent in terms of the violations of human rights.[186] Better still, a careful study of its April 2011 report demonstrates that the situation of the rights of people in Cuba is one of the least unfavorable on the American continent.

Thus demonstrating that the discriminatory and contradictory character of the Common Position is not difficult to do. At the same time, of course, Cuba is not beyond reproach. Amnesty International states that in Cuba "the rights to freedom of expression, association, and assembly remained limited and many critics of one-party rule have been harassed." The organization, in April 2011, points to the presence of eleven prisoners of conscience, who were finally released in November of the same year as part of an agreement between the Cuban government, the Catholic Church, and Spain. According to Amnesty International, there are to date no political prisoners in Cuba.[187] This organization for the defense of the rights of human beings emphasizes that all media are "under state control," with access to cyberspace controlled and "sometimes even blocked." Many opponents have been in custody "before being released several days or weeks later without charge or trial."[188]

To any critical mind, which is a "fundamental pillar of journalism," it is impossible not to see the illegitimacy of the political, diplomatic, and cultural sanctions imposed by the European Union against Cuba. In order to justify its sanctimonious moralizing on the issue of human rights, Brussels must first be blameless in this area. As we will see, this is far from the case.

Amnesty International provides a tough and uncompromising assessment of the situation of human rights in Europe. For Cuba, unlike members of the European Union, it does not report a single case of the following:

- Murder committed by security forces (Austria, Bulgaria, France, Italy, UK, Sweden);
- Murder of children by police (Greece);
- Massive murders of children suffering from mental illness (Bulgaria);
- Torture and inhuman or degrading treatment by the authorities (Austria, Belgium, Spain, France, Greece, Italy, Portugal, Romania, UK, Slovakia);

- Responsibility in a genocide (Belgium);
- Torture and inhuman or degrading treatment by the authorities in the treatment of minors (Belgium, Bulgaria, Denmark);
- Torture supported by the highest level of the state authorities (UK);
- Impunity for security forces guilty of murder (Bulgaria, France, Sweden);
- Impunity for security forces guilty of torture and other ill-treatment (Belgium, Spain);
- Use of evidence obtained by torture (Romania);
- Obstruction of justice and compensation for victims of torture and ill-treatment by the police (Germany);
- Expulsion of people, including minors, to countries that practice torture and where there is a risk of persecution (Austria, Bulgaria, Cyprus, Denmark, Spain, Italy, Malta, Netherlands, UK, Slovakia, Sweden);
- Violent police repression of demonstrations (Belgium, Greece);
- Racist police brutality against foreigners and members of ethnic minorities (Austria);
- Human trafficking and slavery (Cyprus, Greece, Italy, UK);
- Secret detention and transfer of prisoners to countries that practice torture (Germany, Belgium, Lithuania, Romania);
- Forced labor (Cyprus);
- Suicide of a minor in custody (Austria);
- Denial of medical, social and legal support for asylum seekers (Belgium);
- Legal discrimination against ethnic minorities (Belgium, Spain);
- Generalized discrimination against minorities (Bulgaria, Denmark, Greece, Hungary);
- Discrimination against minorities on the part of the courts of justice (Bulgaria);
- Forced expulsion of ethnic minorities as well as the destruction of their homes by the authorities (Bulgaria, Greece, Romania)
- Widespread racist attacks (Bulgaria);

- Recurrent attacks against sexual minorities (Bulgaria, Italy, Slovakia);
- Non-recognition of the rights of sexual minorities by the authorities (Cyprus);
- Police support for the extreme right movements during demonstrations (Cyprus);
- Recurrent violence against women (Denmark, Finland, Malta, Portugal, Sweden);
- Recurrent violence against young girls (Finland, Portugal);
- Corporal punishment against children in specialized centers for minors (Spain);
- Legal impunity for perpetrators of sexual violence against women (Denmark, Finland, Sweden);
- Detention of juveniles in adult prisons (Denmark);
- Detention of asylum-seeking minors (Finland, Netherlands);
- Secret detentions (Spain);
- Ban on investigating crimes that fall under international law (Spain);
- Violations of religious freedom of women (Spain, France, Netherlands);
- Stigmatization of ethnic minorities by the presidents of the republics and the authorities (France, Romania);
- Discriminatory political discourse by authorities (France, Hungary, Italy, Romania, Slovenia);
- Racial discrimination against minorities (Italy, Portugal, Slovenia);
- Lack of access to education and decent housing for ethnic minorities (France, Italy, Portugal);
- Detention under inhumane conditions (Greece, Ireland, Italy)
- Racist violence (Greece, Hungary, Czech Republic);
- Attacks on journalists by the authorities (Greece);
- Violence by authorities against minorities and asylum seekers (Greece);

- Racial segregation in education and exclusion of children from ethnic minorities in the educational system (Greece, Hungary, Italy, Czech Republic, Romania, Slovakia, Slovenia);
- Education of minority children in institutions for the mentally handicapped (Czech Republic);
- Racial segregation in access to health care (Hungary, Italy, Romania, Slovakia, Slovenia);
- Racist crime (Hungary, Czech Republic);
- Impunity for those responsible for racist crimes (Hungary);
- Anti-Semitic crimes (Hungary);
- Crimes against sexual minorities (Hungary);
- Infringement of the rights of children (Ireland);
- Abuse of children (Ireland);
- Death by neglect of children entrusted to public services for the protection of children (Ireland);
- Non-respect for the rights of sexual minorities (Ireland);
- Violation of the rights of asylum seekers (Ireland);
- "Totally unacceptable and inhumane" conditions in hospitals (Ireland);
- Violation of the right to abortion (Ireland);
- Legal prohibition of abortion (Malta);
- Refusal to include torture as a crime punishable under the Penal Code (Italy);
- Discriminatory legislation against sexual minorities with criminalization of homosexuality (Lithuania);
- Discriminatory government policies and practices including ethnic profiling (Netherlands);
- Forced sterilization of minority women (Czech Republic, Slovakia);
- People arbitrarily deleted from population registers (Slovenia);

The factual data highlighted by Amnesty International raise the question of the legitimacy of the European Common Position toward Cuba. They also appear to have escaped the discernment of *El País*. The facts contradict the point of view adopted by the Madrid daily on this issue and illustrate the ambiguous nature of its analyses.

5

The Dissidents

IN TERMS OF INTERNAL political opposition, *El País* notes that the "Group of 75," since released, had been "charged with 'conspiring' with the United States and, in the spring of 2003, sentenced to long prison terms."[189] The newspaper also reports that those convicted had been accused of "engaging in subversive activities and committing crimes against 'national security.'"[190] Finally, the paper recalls that Amnesty International considered them to be "prisoners of conscience."[191]

El País takes typographical precautions by putting quotation marks around the words "conspiring" and "national security" to indicate that these are the charges brought by the Havana government. However, he does not provide details, thereby casting doubt on the basis of these charges. In fact, the Cuban government had accused the dissidents of being financed by a foreign power, namely the United States, in violation of the Cuban Penal Code, which prohibits any citizen from being in the pay of a foreign government.

By consulting official United States government documents, it is easy to verify if these accusations have any basis in fact. *El País* chose to ignore Washington's foreign policy toward Cuba concerning internal dissidents. Washington's declared policy is to achieve regime change in Havana. To accomplish this, U.S. government policy toward Cuba is based on two strategies: economic sanctions and the financing of an internal opposition. From 1959 to 1991, organizing support for internal dissidence remained a secret. Since 1992, it has been public and assertive.

Article 1705 of the Torricelli Act of 1992 states that "the United States will provide assistance to appropriate non-governmental organizations, for the support of individuals and independent non-governmental organizations that promote nonviolent democratic change in Cuba."[192]

Section 109 of the Helms-Burton Act of 1996 confirms this policy: "The President [of the United States] is authorized to offer assistance and offer aid and provide other support for individuals and independent non-governmental organizations in support of democracy-building efforts for Cuba."[193]

The first report of the Commission for Assistance to a Free Cuba foresees the establishment of a "solid support program promoting Cuban civil society." Among the measures recommended is funding at the $36 million level to "support the democratic opposition and strengthen the emerging civil society."[194]

On March 3, 2005, Roger Noriega, then Assistant Secretary for Western Hemisphere Affairs for the Bush administration, said that $14.4 million had been added to the 2004 budget of $36 million. Noriega revealed the identity of some of the people contributing to the development of U.S. foreign policy against Cuba, namely Marta Beatriz Roque, the Ladies in White, and Oswaldo Paya.[195]

The second report of the Commission for Assistance to a Free Cuba foresees a budget of $31 million in increased funding to support internal opposition. In addition, it allocates funding of at least $20 million each and every following year "until the dictatorship ceases to exist."[196] The plan also provides for "training and equipping independent journalists from print, radio, and television media in Cuba."[197]

The U.S. Agency for International Development (USAID), dependent upon the federal government, admits to financing

Cuban dissidents. For the fiscal year 2009, according to the Agency, the amount of aid to Cuban dissidents stood at $15.62 million. "The vast majority of the money is intended for individuals on the ground in Cuba. Our objective is to maximize the amount of support that benefits Cubans on the island."[198]

The USAID underscores the following point: "We have trained hundreds of journalists over a ten-year period whose work has appeared in major international news outlets." This statement undermines claims concerning the allegiances of the "independent journalists" in Cuba. Having been trained by and in the pay of the United States, they serve the interests of Washington whose purpose is, as reported by the official records of the State Department, "regime change" on the island.[199]

From a legal standpoint, this fact places dissidents who accept the compensation offered by the USAID in the position of being agents of a foreign power, a serious violation of Cuba's Penal Code, as well as that of any other country in the world. The Agency, conscious of this reality, points out that "no one is required to accept or take part in any USG programs if they don't want to."[200]

The United States Interest Section (USIS) in Havana confirmed in a statement: "For a long time now, the policy of the United States has been to provide humanitarian assistance to the Cuban people, especially the families of political prisoners."[201] In reference to financial aid, Michael Parmly, former head of USIS, claimed that "the United States is proud to provide assistance to those individuals who in most cases have no one else to turn to."[202]

Laura Pollan, of the dissident group Ladies in White, openly accepted the funding, stating, "We accept aid, support, from either the extreme right or left, without conditions."[203] Regime opponent Vladimiro Roca also confessed that the Cuban dissidents are paid by Washington, stating that the financial assistance received was "totally and completely legal." In terms of the dissident René Gómez, financial support from the United States is "not something that we should hide or be ashamed of."[204] Similarly, the opponent Elizardo Sánchez confirmed the existence of compensation from the United States: "The question is not who sends aid but what is done with it."[205] For her part, Marta Beatriz Roque said that economic aid she receives from the U.S. government is essential to her activities as a dissident.[206]

Agence France-Presse reports that the "dissidents, for their part, claimed and assumed the financial aid."[207] The Spanish news agency EFE refers to "opponents paid by the United States."[208] The British news agency Reuters says, "The U.S. government openly provides federally-funded support for dissident activities, which Cuba considers to be an illegal act."[209] The U.S. news agency the Associated Press acknowledged that the policy of fabricating and financing internal opposition was not new: "Over the years, the U.S. government has spent many millions of dollars to support Cuba's opposition. . . ."[210] It also referred to the lifestyle of the dissidents who benefit from both Washington and the Cuban social system:

> Some American funding comes directly from the United States government whose laws call for ousting Fidel Castro and his younger brother Raúl, Cuba's new president. USAID, which oversees the governmental financial support for a "democratic transition" in Cuba, budgeted more than $33 million for Cuban civil society in this fiscal year [2008].
>
> Nearly all Cubans—dissidents included—have free housing, health care, and education through college. Rations of rice, potatoes, soap, and other commodities get people through part of each month.[211]

The French daily Libération notes that the dissident Guillermo Fariñas "has never denied receiving 'gifts' from the U.S. Interests Section that have allowed him to obtain a computer and do his job as an 'independent journalist' on the Internet."[212]

A document classified as "confidential," but published by WikiLeaks, confirms this sort of financing. It was sent by the USIS in Havana to the State Department. In it, Jonathan D. Farrar, then head of the U.S. diplomatic corps in Havana, "seeks approval of funding from the Human Rights Defenders Fund [HRDF] for certain groups and individuals in Cuba," citing specifically the Ladies in White. According to Farrar, "Humanitarian assistance should be given to them according to the OFAC regulations that govern exports to Cuba." He references a budget of "$5,000," an amount that is equivalent to 27 years of the average salary in Cuba. Farrar is, however, well aware of the illegal nature of this funding and recalls in the memorandum that "the receipt of funds from a foreign source makes anyone liable to prosecution and imprisonment under Law 88."[213]

For its part, Amnesty International admits that the people it considers to be "political prisoners" were sentenced "for receiving funds or equipment from the U.S. government for activities perceived by the authorities as subversive or doing harm to Cuba."[214] Although *El País* does not fail to remind us of the status that Amnesty International assigned to these individuals, it chose to remain silent on certain details in their regard that raise a number of questions.

In fact, Jonathan D. Farrar, former head of the United States Interests Section in Havana, revealed that certain U.S. allies, including Canada, do not share Amnesty International's position on the question of "political prisoners." He recalled a discussion with his Canadian counterparts: "Our Canadian colleagues asked us the following question: 'Should someone who takes money from the United States be considered a political prisoner?'" They pointed out that all Western nations sanction, in the same manner, individuals who are funded by a foreign power with the aim of overthrowing the established order.[215]

This view is shared by other European diplomats, who spoke out during a meeting with Farrar: "The representatives of the European Union present at the meeting discredited dissidents in the same terms as those used by the government of Cuba, insisting that 'they do not represent anyone.'"[216] They added that the dissidents "do not have any influence within Cuban society and offer no political alternative to the Government of Cuba." For Farrar,

"There are few, if any, dissidents who have a political vision that could be useful to a future government. Although the dissidents fail to admit it, they are very slightly known in Cuba outside of the foreign diplomatic and press corps. . . . It is highly unlikely that they could play a significant role in any government that might succeed the Castro brothers."[217]

The U.S. diplomat suggests another reason: the continued popularity of Fidel Castro with Cubans some fifty years after having come to power. "It would be a mistake to underestimate . . . popular support for the government, particularly that emanating from working class communities and students."[218] Farrar underscored "the significant admiration for Fidel" within Cuban society.[219]

Moreover, despite the political, economic, media, and financial resources made available to the Cuban opposition, it has always been cut off from any grassroots base. It is deeply divided and aging rapidly. These are the conclusions drawn by Jonathan D. Farrar in a confidential memorandum to the State Department dated April 15, 2009, titled "The United States and the Role of the Opposition in Cuba."[220]

The diplomat first noted that Cuban president Raúl Castro currently holds "a position of unquestioned authority." Regarding the role of dissent, he states that it is "null and void" because "opposition groups are dominated by individuals with strong egos who do not work well together." Farrar also said that "the dissident movement in Cuba is aging and completely disconnected from the lives of ordinary Cubans." It is also clear that, because of the payments they receive, Cuban dissidents lead a lifestyle that no average citizen of the island could afford.[221]

Farrar acknowledges that he is in regular contact "with most of the official dissident movements in Havana," the members of which frequently visit the U.S. Interests Section. However, "There is no evidence to show that the dominant dissident organizations in Cuba have any influence over average Cubans. Informal surveys of visa applicants and asylum seekers showed virtually no knowledge of dissident personalities or their agenda."[222]

Farrar says that this may be explained by the age of opponents, most of whom are between fifty and seventy, citing Francisco Chaviano, Rene Gomez Manzano and Oswaldo Paya. "They have little contact with younger Cubans, and their message does not resonate with this segment of society." The diplomat deplores the infighting among different groups and their lack of unity. His judgment is implacable: "Despite claims that they represent 'thousands of Cubans,' we have no evidence that such support exists, at least not here in Havana where we are stationed." He adds that "they have no influence over Cuban society and offer no alternative policies to the government of Cuba."[223]

There is a reason for this, and it is to be found in the Cuban character.[224] Cuban society is certainly far from monolithic, and dissatisfied sectors of the population are harsh in their criticism of the authorities when it comes to exposing the contradictions and aberrations, bigotry, and injustices that the Cuban system sometimes generates. The criticisms are often harsh and uncompromising and, according to Farrar, these criticisms are reported in the Cuban media. USIS notes that "a lot of press articles are very critical of current policies."[225] Nevertheless, despite all of the daily vicissitudes, Cubans remain deeply attached to their independence and national sovereignty and cannot conceive that their compatriots could accept to be in the service of a foreign power that has always dreamed of repossessing the island. This attitude is accounted for by the "anti-imperialist" political legacy left by the great men of the nation's history, men such as José Martí, Antonio Maceo, Maximo Gomez, Julio Antonio Mella, Antonio Guiteras, Eduardo Chibás, and Fidel Castro.

USIS also criticizes the lack of a program and the greed of the dissidents, who seem uniquely interested in the revenue that can be made in the dissident trade:

> Their greatest effort is to garner enough resources to ensure that the main organizers and their supporters live well. One political organization openly and frankly maintained that it

needed money to pay salaries and presented a budget in the
hope that USIS might fund it. In addition to fundraising, their
main concern, their second priority seems to be that of criti-
cizing or marginalizing the activities of their competitors in
order to preserve their own power and access to resources.[226]

Farrar again stresses the importance of the opposition in the
realization of U.S. objectives. "We need to support them," he says,
while seeking an alternative to reinvigorate the dissident movement in Cuba.[227]

The U.S. diplomat notes that the objective is "to support the
good work of the dissident movement" in its campaign against the
Havana government, suggesting that this can be done by focusing
on the duel themes of "human rights" and "political prisoners,"
the two reasons given by Washington for maintaining economic
sanctions against Cuba. However, the campaign is primarily for
international public opinion because it "does not interest Cubans
whose main concern is to achieve a higher standard of living and
increased opportunities to travel."[228]

U.S. diplomacy has no illusions about the effectiveness of its
economic sanctions against the island, sanctions that have plunged
the country into a difficult economic crisis. Farrar concedes that
"the Cuban people have grown accustomed to tough times and will
respond to future government belt tightening with similar endur-
ance."[229] He rules out the possibility of a serious crisis and notes
that "Cuba and Cubans are not as vulnerable as they were in 1989
before the end of Soviet subsidies." Moreover, "the standard of
living of Cubans, even if it is not as high as it was twenty years ago,
before the end of Soviet aid, is still much better than during the
darkest days of the period between 1990 and 1993 when the GDP
fell by more than 35%." In addition, "Today's Cuban economy is
less vulnerable . . . through more diversified sources of income and
credits and a Cuban population with more resources."[230]

Despite the economic sanctions imposed by Washington, the U.S.
diplomat suggests that Cubans feel no particular animosity against

Americans as a people because they do not consider the North American public responsible for Washington's policies. USIS emphasizes Cuban's "positive feelings toward the American people."[231]

Wayne S. Smith, the last U.S. citizen to have been stationed in Cuba with the rank of ambassador, confirmed the subversive nature of U.S. policy, stating that it is "illegal and unwise to send money to the Cuban dissidents."[232] He added that "no one should give money to the dissidents, much less for the purpose of overthrowing the Cuban government," for "when the United States declares its objective is to overthrow the Cuban government, and later admits that one of the means of achieving that goal is to provide funds to Cuban dissidents, these dissidents find themselves de facto in the position of agents paid by a foreign power to overthrow their own government."[233]

The Madrid daily also mentioned the case of the Damas de Blanco (Ladies in White), a dissident group composed of the wives and daughters of "political" prisoners, who regularly hold protest marches to demand the release of their relatives. Following an agreement between Havana, Madrid, and the Catholic Church, all of these prisoners were released between July and November 2011. Far from putting an end to their activities, the Ladies in White are now demanding the release of people convicted of violent crimes and terrorist activities.

Unlike *El País*, which chose not to disclose this information, the BBC in London has not failed to notice this contradiction: "The prisoners were all released over the past year under an agreement brokered by the Roman Catholic Church, and some have gone into exile in Spain. But the Ladies in White have continued to campaign for the release of around fifty other prisoners who have been convicted of violent crimes, such as hijacking, which they say are political."[234]

For its part, the U.S. Associated Press noted that some of the prisoners "would not normally be seen as political prisoners. . . . But a closer look will find bombers, hijackers and intelligence agents" on the list. The report said that "about half were convicted of terrorism, hijacking, and other violent crimes, and four of them are former military or intelligence agents convicted of espionage or revealing state secrets."[235] Some have made armed incursions into Cuba and at least two, Humberto Eladio Real Suarez and Ernesto Cruz León, are responsible for the deaths of civilians, in 1994 and in 1997.[236]

Ricardo Alarcón, president of the Cuban Parliament, did not fail to highlight these contradictions: "Curiously, our critics talk about a list [and not about names]. Why do they not admit that they are, in fact, asking for the freedom of the person who killed Fabio di Celmo?,"[237] a young Italian tourist who died in a 1997 bomb attack on a Havana hotel.

For its part, Amnesty International says it cannot consider these persons to be "prisoners of conscience" because they are "people brought to trial for terrorism and espionage. Among them are those who have tried, or even succeeded in blowing up hotels. . . . We certainly do not ask for their release and will not describe them as prisoners of conscience."[238]

This position is shared by the Spanish government, which played a key role in the release of the so-called political prisoners. Miguel Moratinos, Spanish Minister of Foreign Affairs, has been quite clear about this: "Don't say that 300 prisoners should be released because there are no 300 prisoners. A week before I arrived, the list from the Commission on Human Rights in Cuba said there were 202. Upon my arrival in Cuba, I found that it had said the day before that there were 167."[239]

The Cuban Catholic Church, through Jaime Ortega y Alamino, Archbishop of Havana, has expressed the same view. He said in October 2011 that the issue of political prisoners was closed since all persons enjoying such status had been released.[240]

The Spanish news agency EFE, one of the news sources used by *El País*, reports that "Cuba has released all of the prisoners designated by Amnesty International as prisoners of conscience."[241]

Once again, *El País* chose not to report to its readers all of the facts concerning Cuban dissidents. The testimonies of the highest Western diplomatic authorities present in Havana, as well as important official primary source documents contradict the view of the Spanish daily. They shed a merciless light on the selective nature of the information published by the newspaper, information aimed at influencing public opinion by revealing only a part of the history of the Cuban dissident movement.

6

Yoani Sánchez

IN 2008, *EL PAÍS* chose to grant the Ortega y Gasset Prize of 15,000 euros to the Cuban dissident Yoani Sánchez. This award is usually given only to writers and journalists with long and prestigious literary careers. This was the first time a person with Sánchez's profile had received such a distinction.[242]

After naming Sánchez in 2009 as one of the one hundred most influential people in Latin America—to the surprise of almost everyone—the Madrid newspaper decided to make her its permanent correspondent in Havana. Her articles are regularly published on both the paper's website and in hard copy.[243] In doing so, the newspaper broke its vaunted promise of impartiality, siding with someone who opposes the government in Havana. Respect for plurality would require that space also be given to a blogger who supports the revolutionary process in order to provide the reader with a more balanced view of Cuban reality.

The brief biography of Yoani Sánchez provided by the newspaper is also problematic. According to *El País*, she is "a Cuban journalist and author of the blog *Generación Y.*"[244] The reader will not learn more. However, it seems important to point out that Yoani Sánchez is a fierce opponent of the government in Havana and shares not only the positions taken by Washington, but also by the U.S. diplomats in Cuba.

THE STORY OF YOANI SÁNCHEZ

Yoani Maria Sánchez Cordero was born in Havana in 1975, graduating with a degree in philology in 2000. After working in the publishing sector and teaching Spanish to tourists, she chose to leave the country with her son. On August 26, 2002, after having married a German named Karl G., she decided to emigrate to Switzerland with a "license to travel abroad," valid for eleven months, because of the "disenchantment and economic strangulation prevailing in Cuba."[245]

During the summer of 2004, two years after leaving the country, she decided to abandon Switzerland, one of the richest nations in the world, and return to Cuba. This choice has raised certain questions to which Sánchez has responded. According to her, the decision was taken for "family reasons and against the advice of a number of friends and family."[246] She did not provide any further details.

On Yoani Sánchez's blog, the situation in Cuba is described as both grotesque and tragic. No positive aspects of Cuban society are divulged. Only aberrations, injustices, contradictions, and difficulties are recounted. Therefore it is difficult to understand why the young Cuban might have decided to leave a wealthy Switzerland to return to live in what appears to be akin to Dante's Inferno, where "pockets are empty and frustration and fear are on the rise everywhere."[247] On her blog, comments about this decision flourish: "I do not understand your return. Why did you not choose to give your son a better future?" "Dear friend, I would like to know why you decided to return to Cuba."[248]

In a note posted to her blog in July 2007, Yoani Sánchez recounts in detail the story of her return to Cuba. "Three years ago in Zurich with my son, I decided to return to live in my own country," stressing that it was "a simple story of an emigrant returning to her home country." She notes, "We bought round-trip tickets." Sánchez nonetheless decided to stay and not return to Switzerland. "My friends thought I was playing a joke on them and my mother refused to believe that her daughter no longer lived in the land of milk and chocolate." On August 12, 2004, Sánchez appeared before the provincial Office of Immigration services in Havana to explain the reasons for her return. "You can imagine my surprise when I was told to line up in the queue of those who had decided to return home. . . . Here I discovered other 'crazy' people like me, all with their truculent homecoming stories."[249]

The case of Sánchez is far from an isolated one, as this anecdote and the comments left on her blog illustrate. More and more Cubans who have emigrated choose to return to their country of origin after having faced many problems adapting to life abroad and having found that the Western El Dorado was perhaps less brilliant than they had imagined—and that the privileges available to them in their home country did not exist elsewhere.

However, beyond the "family reasons" she cites, Yoani Sánchez fails to tell the real reasons that led her to return to Cuba. According to the archives of the Cuban consulate in Bern, her time in Switzerland was actually more difficult than expected. Sánchez discovered a Western lifestyle different from that to which she was accustomed in Cuba, where, despite the daily difficulties and vicissitudes, all citizens have a relatively balanced diet even with the ration book and shortages, access to care, education, culture, and free entertainment, as well as housing and a safe atmosphere. In Switzerland, Sánchez had great difficulty finding a job and leading a decent life. Desperate, she decided to go home and explain the reasons for her return to the authorities. According to them, Sánchez begged immigration authorities to grant her a special dispensation that would "revoke her emigration status," something that was done.[250]

THE BLOG *GENERACIÓN Y*

In April 2007, Yoani Sánchez decided to join the world of the Cuban opposition by creating *Generación Y*.[251] In the blog, her criticisms of the government are often harsh and lacking in nuance. She presents an apocalyptic view of Cuban reality and accuses the authorities of being responsible for all of its ills. According to her, Cuba is "a huge prison with ideological walls,"[252] "a disaster that has lasted for 50 years,"[253] "a boat taking water on every side that is on the verge of sinking,"[254] a country "where shadow beings, like vampires, feed on our human joy," "where we inoculate fear through beatings, threats, blackmail."[255] Yoani Sánchez describes Cuban reality as terrifying, a portrait in which no positive trait ever emerges. She also holds her compatriots in low esteem, suggesting that "80%" of them are driven by "opportunism."[256] According to Sánchez, in Cuba "the process, the system, the expectations and the illusions have suffered a shipwreck." "It's a total wreck," she announces before concluding with this pithy metaphor: "The boat has already sunk." For her, it is clear that Cuba must change direction and government: "The helmsman and the entire crew"[257] must go in order to establish a "capitalism sui generis."[258]

Similarly, Yoani Sánchez avoids mentioning the extraordinary geopolitical context that Cuba has found itself in since 1959. She minimizes the impact of the economic sanctions—"an excuse" used by the Cuban government—claiming that "the Cuban government is responsible for 80% of the current economic crisis with 20% due to the economic sanctions."[259] According to her, "The blockade constitutes the perfect argument for the Cuban government to maintain intolerance, control, and internal repression. If sanctions were lifted tomorrow, I doubt that we would see the effects."[260] The sanctions "are used to justify the economic disaster as well as repression against those who think differently."[261]

Recognizing that Washington's objective is the overthrow of the Cuban government, she admits unashamedly to sharing the same goal: "The United States wants a change of government in Cuba. This is what I also want."[262] Similarly, Yoani Sánchez vilifies "the supposedly free medical care and the supposedly free education" that she sees as mere propaganda slogans of the Cuban regime.[263]

According to her, the social gains of the Cuban system are exaggerated because "they were already in place" in Cuba years prior to the Revolution. She does not hide her sympathy for the Batista dictatorship that was overthrown in 1959 by Fidel Castro's rebels. Under it, "there was a free, open and pluralistic press and radio broadcasts that covered the political spectrum."[264]

COUNTLESS WELL-REMUNERATED PRIZES

El País obscures the fact that never has any dissident in Cuba—perhaps in the world—received so many international awards in such a short time, awards that carry with them certain advantages: they have brought in enough money to allow Yoani Sánchez to live comfortably in Cuba until the end of her days. Indeed, the blogger has received in total up to 250,000 euros, that is to say, a sum equivalent to more than twenty years of minimum wage in a country such as France, one of the world's richest nations. The minimum monthly wage in Cuba is 420 pesos, that is, $18 or 14 euros; thus Yoani Sánchez has been awarded the equivalent of 1,488 years of minimum wage in Cuba for her dissident activities.[265] However, Sánchez is an unknown quantity in her own country, as she candidly admits: "*Time* magazine included me in its list of the most influential people in 2008 along with 99 other celebrities, even though I have never appeared on stage or in a forum. My neighbors do not even know if 'Yoani' is spelled with an 'h' in the middle or an 's' at the end. . . . I guess the others on the list are asking: Who is this unknown Cuban blogger who is listed among us?"[266] The U.S. magazine apparently used political and ideological criteria when selecting Sánchez, something that inevitably casts a shadow of doubt over the credibility of their rankings. This line of reasoning seems valid for the other awards as well.

In 2009, in violation of the legislation on economic sanctions, the U.S. Treasury Department ordered the closure of more than eighty websites that promote trade with Cuba. Curiously, the website of Yoani Sánchez was spared, even though it promotes the sale of her book in Italian and offers the possibility of paying for it through PayPal, a system no Cuban living in Cuba is able to use because of the economic sanctions that prohibit, among other things, e-commerce. Similarly, Sánchez has a copyright for her blog: "© 2009 Generation Y—All Rights Reserved." No other Cuban blogger can do this because of the laws governing the embargo. Sánchez registered her domain name through the U.S. company GoDaddy, whose main feature is anonymity. The Pentagon also uses this service to record sites discreetly. How is it that Yoani Sánchez, a Cuban blogger living in Cuba, can register her site with a U.S. company when this is strictly forbidden by the legislation governing economic sanctions?[267]

In addition, the *Generación Y* site of Yoani Sánchez is extremely sophisticated, with entries for Facebook and Twitter. It receives 14 million visits per month and is the only site in the world to be available in no less than 18 languages (English, French, Spanish, Italian, German, Portuguese, Russian, Slovenian, Polish, Chinese, Japanese, Lithuanian, Czech, Bulgarian, Dutch, Finnish, Hungarian, Korean, and Greek). No other site in the world, including those of the most important international institutions, for example the United Nations, the World Bank, the International Monetary Fund, the OECD, and the European Union, has as many language versions. Neither does the U.S. State Department site, nor even the CIA site, possess such variety.[268]

Another aspect is surprising. The site that hosts Sánchez's blog has a bandwidth 60 times greater than what Cuba makes available for all of its Internet users! Other questions inevitably arise: Who administers these pages in 18 languages? Who pays the directors and translators who work daily on Sánchez' site? How much are they paid? In addition, management of more than 14 million site visits per month is extremely expensive. It would be interesting to know who is responsible for these costs.[269]

CLOSE TIES WITH U.S. DIPLOMACY

Yoani Sánchez also maintains close relations with the U.S. diplomatic corps in Cuba, something revealed through a cable from USIS that was classified "secret" because of its sensitive content, but later made public by WikiLeaks. She is held in high esteem by the Obama administration, something made evident by her secret meeting with U.S. Deputy Secretary of State Bisa Williams, which took place in the young Cuban blogger's apartment during Williams's visit to Cuba September 16–20, 2010. Although Sánchez regularly discusses her daily schedule on her blog, there is no hint of her meeting with Williams, an omission that illustrates the clandestine nature of this encounter. The diplomatic cable also reveals the links between the media-seeking Cuban blogger and the U.S. representatives in Havana, as well as the importance placed upon the dissident by Washington. [270]

In this regard, Michael Parmly, former head of the U.S. Interests Section in Havana, as shown in confidential documents, met regularly with Yoani Sánchez in his personal diplomatic residence.[271] He expressed concern about the release of U.S. diplomatic cables by WikiLeaks: "I would be really annoyed if the many conversations I had with Yoani Sánchez came to be published. She could pay with her life."[272] Why might Yoani Sánchez be in trouble with the Cuban justice system if her actions, as she maintains, respect the limits of the law?

In 2009, *El País* widely publicized the interview that U.S. president Barack Obama granted Yoani Sánchez, something considered quite exceptional. The blogger stated that she had sent a similar questionnaire to Cuban president Raúl Castro who, according to her, had not deigned to respond. However, confidential documents from USIS, released by WikiLeaks, challenge these statements. They reveal that in fact it was an official of the U.S. diplomatic mission in Havana who was responsible for preparing responses for the dissident and not President Obama himself.

More serious, however, is learning that Yoani Sánchez, contrary to her assertions, never sent a questionnaire to Raúl Castro. The head of USIS, Jonathan D. Farrar, confirmed this in a letter sent to the State Department: "She did not expect an answer from him, because she said that [the questions] were never sent to the Cuban President."[273]

THE TWITTER ACCOUNT OF YOANI SÁNCHEZ

In addition to her website *Generación Y*, Yoani Sánchez has a Twitter account and claims more than 214,000 followers,[274] only 32 of whom actually live in Cuba. For her part, the Cuban dissident claims to follow more than 80,000 people. On her profile, Sánchez presents herself as "a blogger, I live in Havana and tell my reality through tweets of 140 characters. I tweet via SMS without access to the Internet."[275]

Yoani Sánchez's version of the facts is hardly credible. It is clearly impossible in Cuba to follow more than 80,000 people through nothing more than SMS or a weekly connection to the Internet from a hotel. Daily access to the Web is essential in order to do this.

Popularity on the Twitter social network is dependent upon your number of followers. The higher the number, the more the account gains in exposure. Similarly, there is a strong correlation between the number of people followed and the visibility of one's own account. The technique used to monitor multiple accounts is commonly used for commercial purposes as well as by politicians during election campaigns.

The Followerwonk.com site permits profile analyses of the fans of all members of the Twitter community. The case study of Yoani Sánchez is revealing in several respects. An analysis of the figures of the Cuban blogger's Twitter account made through the site reveals, from 2010 on, an impressive amount of activity on Yoani Sánchez's account. Beginning in June 2010, Sánchez averaged connecting with over 200 Twitter accounts per day, with peaks of up to 700 in a 24-hour period. Unless you spend hours on the Internet at this—which seems highly unlikely—it is impossible to subscribe to that many accounts in such a short period of time. It seems therefore apparent that these subscriptions were generated by computer.[276]

Similarly, it was found that nearly 50,000 of Yoani Sánchez's followers are actually inactive or shadow accounts, which create the illusion that the Cuban blogger enjoys great popularity on the social networks. In fact, of the 214,063 profiles on the Twitter account @yoanisanchez, 27,012 are empty shells (without photos) and 20,600 have the characteristics of shadow accounts because of their nonexistent network activity (0–3 tweets sent since the account's creation).

Thus, among the shadow accounts that follow Yoani Sánchez on Twitter, 3,363 have no followers themselves, and 2,897 follow only the Sánchez account and possibly one or two others. Similarly, certain accounts exhibit rather strange characteristics: they have no fans, follow only Yoani Sánchez, but nonetheless have issued over 2,000 tweets.

This operation, designed to create a fictitious popularity on Twitter, is impossible to perform without Internet access. It also requires technological support and a substantial budget. According to an article in the Mexican daily *La Jornada*, titled "El ciberacarreo, la nueva estrategia de los políticos on Twitter," a survey of this sort of transaction implicates Mexican presidential candidates. Many companies based in the United States, Asia, and Latin America offer this fictional popularity service at high prices. For an army of 25,000 followers invented on Twitter, one pays up to $2,000, and for 500 profiles used by 50 people, the price fluctuates between $12,000 and $15,000.[277]

Yoani Sánchez sends an average of 9.3 tweets per day. In 2011, the blogger published about 400 tweets per month. The price of a tweet in Cuba is one convertible peso (CUC = $.85), representing a total of 400 CUC monthly. The minimum wage in Cuba is 420 Cuban pesos, that is, about 16 CUC. Yoani Sánchez spends each month the equivalent of twenty-five months of minimum salary in Cuba.

By comparison, in France the minimum wage is around 1,000 euros. Thus the blogger in Cuba spends an amount equivalent to 25,000 euros per month on Twitter, that is, 300,000 euros every year. Where do the resources required to pay for these activities come from?

Other questions inevitably arise. How many people actually follow the activities of the Cuban oppositionist on the social network? Who funds the creation of these fictitious accounts? For what purpose? What interests are behind the figure of Yoani Sánchez? Why does *El País*, which published a study on shadow accounts that it qualifies as "fraudulent," remain silent on the Twitter account of Yoani Sánchez?[278]

THE PURCHASING POWER OF YOANI SÁNCHEZ

Yoani Sánchez has a very narrow vision of her country, a vision she shares on her *Generación Y* blog. Here, Cuban reality is described in apocalyptic terms, and she reports daily activities composed of suffering and deprivation. She strongly criticizes the Havana government, which she accuses of being responsible for all of these ills.

"My son asks me if there will be something to eat today," she notes in a June 29, 2012, column, stating that this situation is occurring "in a society where every personal initiative is surrounded by obstacles and impediments, especially if it occurs independently."[279] She claims to struggle daily against "the obstacles of life."[280]

She claims even to have trouble feeding her own son, "faced with the hierarchy of a totalitarian government"[281] that uses "the eternal foreign threat to disqualify the dissatisfied."[282] Thus "a few pennies increase in the price of food is enough to make the thermometer that measures the daily anguish and anxiety levels explode."[283]

Upon reading these lines, one has the impression that the young Cuban dissident is going hungry and is in a state of utter destitution. But her statements hardly stand up under analysis. Far from living in poverty, Yoani Sánchez enjoys privileged material conditions compared to the vast majority of her countrymen. In the July 23, 2012 edition of *El País*, we discover that the blogger has written a critique of the "10 best restaurants that serve the new Cuban cuisine."[284]

Transformed into a gourmet food critic, Sánchez ranks the top ten restaurants in the Cuban capital and describes in detail the succulent menus that may be enjoyed for an average price of "20 euros," that is, the equivalent of one month's salary in Cuba. Thus, the Café Laurent, the Decamerón, the Habana Chef, La Casa, La Mimosa, La Moneda Cubana, Le Chansonnier, Mamma Mia, Rancho Blanco, and Río Mar win the competition.

Several questions inevitably come to mind. In order to establish a hierarchical classification that could be taken a bit seriously, the young dissident had to go, at the very least, to fifty restaurants in Havana whose meals cost an average of 20 euros. How could Yoani Sánchez, who claims to have difficulty feeding her son, spend 1,000 euros, an amount that represents the equivalent of four years' average salary in Cuba (!), to patronize the most exclusive restaurants in the Cuban capital? Why would a person claiming to be interested in the fate of her fellow citizens undertake a report on the most upscale restaurants in Cuba, restaurants few Cubans can afford?

The image that Yoani Sánchez presents of herself—that of a fragile woman fighting against an all-powerful state and laboring under serious material difficulties—hardly conforms to the reality of her situation. Indeed, this figurehead of the Cuban dissident movement enjoys a standard of living that almost no other Cuban on the island can afford.

The Inter American Press Association (IAPA), which includes the major private media conglomerates on the continent, decided to appoint her regional vice president of the Freedom of the Press

Committee in Cuba.[285] Sánchez, usually so prolific on her blog, has kept a tight silence about her new role. There is a reason for this: her remuneration. The Cuban dissident now earns a salary of $6,000 per month after taxes (and this figure excludes the 250,000 euros she has received as recipient of different prizes). This is a very comfortable income, one usually reserved for senior executives in the richest nations. The importance of salary is even more obvious in that Yoani Sánchez resides in a third world country, a welfare state, where commodities are heavily subsidized.

In Cuba, there is a dual currency system: the CUC and the CUP. The CUC is worth about $.80 or 25 CUP. Thus, with her salary from the IAPA, Yoani Sánchez has an income the equivalent of 4,800 CUC or 120,000 CUP.

We now evaluate the purchasing power of this Cuban dissident. With such a salary, Yoani Sánchez can afford to purchase any of what follows:

- 300,000 bus tickets;
- 6,000 taxi trips throughout greater Havana[286];
- 60,000 movie tickets;
- 24,000 theater tickets;
- 6,000 new books;
- 24,000 per month rent for a type F3 apartment in Havana[287];
- 120,000 glasses of guarapo (cane juice);
- 12,000 hamburgers;
- 12,000 pizzas;
- 9,600 beers;
- 17,142 packs of cigarettes;
- 12,000 pounds of rice;
- 8,000 packages of spaghetti;
- 10,000 pounds of sugar;
- 24,000 scoops of ice cream;
- 40,000 liters of yogurt;
- 5,000 pounds of beans;
- 120,000 liters of milk (if she has a child under 7 years of age);

- 120,000 cups of coffee;
- 80,000 eggs;
- 60,000 pounds of chicken;
- 60,000 pounds of pork;
- 24,000 pounds of bananas;
- 12,000 pounds of oranges;
- 12,000 pounds of onions;
- 20,000 pounds of tomatoes;
- 24,000 tubes of toothpaste;
- 24,000 bars of soap;
- 1,333,333 kilowatts/hour of electricity[288];
- 357,142 cubic meters of drinking water[289];
- 1,090,910 cubic meters of gas[290];
- 4,800 liters of gasoline;
- An unlimited number of visits to the doctor, dentist, eye doctor, or other health professional, as these services are free for all Cubans;
- An unlimited number of registrations for courses on sport, drama, music, etc. (also free).

These figures reflect the real living standards of Yoani Sánchez and cast a dark cloud over the credibility of the Cuban dissident. In light of all these facts, it is inevitable that doubts arise concerning the credibility of Yoani Sánchez, doubts that *El País*, which has assumed responsibility for her international media exposure, did not bother to point out.[291]

Designating Yoani Sánchez, a declared opponent of the Cuban government, as its resident collaborator in Havana, *El País* has broken with the covenant of impartiality essential to any journalistic activity. By taking a stand against the Cuban authorities, it has abandoned the field of information provision for political profit, all to the detriment of its duty toward citizens.

7

The Case of the Five Cuban Political Prisoners

IN AN ARTICLE PUBLISHED in 2010, *El País* turned to the case of the five Cuban intelligence officers—Gerardo Hernández Nordelo, Ramón Labañino Salazar, Fernando González Llort, Antonio Guerrero, and René González Rodríguez Sehweret—who have been incarcerated in the United States since 1998. The Five, as they are known to Cubans, were sentenced to long prison terms for having infiltrated groups of violent Cuban exiles in Florida responsible for terrorist attacks against the island. The newspaper discussed these reasons but carefully noted that this is merely Havana's point of view. It added that the Five were "accused of espionage."[292]

In another article dated September 30, 2011, *El País* emphasizes that they were convicted "of espionage."[293] On October 7, 2011, the newspaper reported that their "mission was to infiltrate and inform Havana on United States military installations in South Florida."[294]

However, all of these statements are incorrect. *El País* failed to report the real story of the Cuban Five. It also ignored the reality of nearly half a century of terrorist attacks against Cuba emanating from the United States.

Since the triumph of the Revolution in 1959, the United States, in an effort to overthrow Fidel Castro, has subjected Cuba to an intense terrorist campaign. According to declassified Washington documents, between October 1960 and April 1961 the CIA introduced more than 75 tons of explosives and 45 tons of weapons into Cuba. In the space of seven months, 110 dynamite attacks were conducted, more than 200 bombs exploded, six trains derailed, 150 factories burned, and some 800 fires set in sugarcane plantations. The CIA funded nearly 300 paramilitary groups, which represented a total of some 4,000 individuals.[295]

In 1971, the CIA used chemical and biological agents against Cuba, including the introduction of swine fever. The swine fever attack resulted in the deaths of half a million head of livestock, the island's main source of protein. In 1981, the CIA introduced dengue hemorrhagic fever into Cuba. It claimed 344,203 victims and killed 158 people, including 101 children.[296]

On October 6, 1976, Luis Posada Carriles and Orlando Bosch, former CIA agents, committed the first act of air terrorism in the history of the American continent when they caused the midair explosion of a Cubana Airlines passenger jet over Barbados. In total, 73 people were killed, including the entire Cuban junior fencing team that had just won the Pan American Games.[297]

Orlando Bosch, now deceased, was never indicted for the Barbados bombing that resulted in the deaths of 73 people. However, proof of his guilt is not lacking. A 1989 report by the Department of Justice noted the following: Bosch has "expressed and demonstrated on several occasions a desire to indiscriminately wound and kill." Joe Whitley, then Acting Associate Attorney General, underscored in his report the reasons for which Bosch, who was serving a prison sentence in the United States for having conducted a bazooka attack against a Polish boat in Miami Bay, was to be deported upon his release from prison: "The explosion of the Cuban civilian airliner on October 6, 1976 was a CORU [Coordination of United Revolutionary Organizations] operation under the direction of Bosch." But he was not deported to Cuba as

Whitley had wished. On July 20, 1990, George H. W. Bush, at the request of the Miami Cuban lobby, chose to grant him a presidential pardon. Shortly thereafter, in gratitude, his son Jeb Bush was elected governor of Florida.[298]

Orlando Bosch has never denied his terrorist past. On April 5, 2006, Bosch was interviewed by reporter Juan Manuel Cao of Miami's Channel 41:

Juan Manuel Cao: Did you shoot down this plane in 1976?

Orlando Bosch: If I tell you that I was involved, I would be implicating myself, and if I tell you that I am not responsible, you would say that I am a liar. Therefore, I will neither confirm nor deny my participation.

Juan Manuel Cao: In this action, 76 [actually 73] people were killed.

Orlando Bosch: Look, chico, in the war that we freedom-loving Cubans are waging against the tyrant, you have to shoot down planes, you have to sink ships, you must be prepared to attack anything that is within your reach.

Juan Manuel Cao: Have you no remorse for those who were killed in this act, for their families?

Orlando Bosch: Who was on board? Four members of the Communist Party, five North Koreans, five [in fact, eleven] Guyanese. Shit, chico, four members of the Communist Party! Who was on board? Our enemies!

Juan Manuel Cao: And the fencers? The young kids on board?

Orlando Bosch: I was in Caracas. I saw those young girls on television. There were six. At the end of the competition, the team captain dedicated their triumph to the tyrant. She gave a speech that was very respectful of the tyrant. We had already agreed in Santo Domingo that everyone coming from Cuba who had glorified the tyrant should run the same risks as those who had fought on the side of this tyranny.

Juan Manuel Cao: If you were to meet the victims' families, would you not find it difficult—

Orlando Bosch: No, because at the end of the day those who were present should have known that they were cooperating with the Cuban tyranny.[299]

In 1997, a wave of terrorist attacks struck the Cuban tourist industry, claiming dozens of victims. Fabio di Celmo, a young Italian tourist, was killed in a bomb explosion in the Copacabana Hotel. On July 12, 1998, in an interview in the *New York Times*, Luis Posada Carriles claimed intellectual responsibility for the 1997 attacks. According to him, "That Italian was sitting in the wrong place at the wrong time." He expressed no regret, saying, "I sleep like a baby." Posada Carriles was never indicted for his terrorist activities and today leads a peaceful life in Miami under the protection of the United States, which refuses either to judge him or extradite him to Cuba or Venezuela, where, in the 1970s, he had also committed crimes. Yet the government of the United States recognizes "the significant criminal history" of Posada Carriles "and the violence in which innocent civilians died," as well as the danger he poses to the national security of the United States and the community.[300]

Posada Carriles's guilt is not in doubt. In addition to the interview in the *New York Times* and his Washington declaration, FBI and CIA archives, declassified in 2005 and 2006 respectively, qualify Posada Carriles as "the hemisphere's worst terrorist." Furthermore, Posada Carriles openly proclaims his terrorist agenda in his autobiography, titled *Los caminos del guerrero* (published in English as *Peaceful Warrior*).[301]

From 1959 to 1997, the United States made no fewer than 5,780 terrorist attacks against Cuba that cost the lives of 3,478 people and caused 2,099 others to fall ill. Fidel Castro himself has been the victim of 637 assassination attempts. The vast majority of these attacks were prepared in Florida by extreme right-wing elements of the Cuban community, which for decades had been organized and financed by the CIA. They acted with impunity because they benefited historically from Washington's protection.[302]

In the early 1990s, faced with the upsurge of these terrorist acts, Cuba decided to send several of its agents to infiltrate exile sectors involved in the violence. By warning Havana authorities in time, these agents were able to prevent almost 170 attacks against Cuba.[303]

In June 1998, thanks to the work of the Cuban agents embedded in Florida, the Havana government put together a voluminous file on 64 Florida residents who were implicated in terrorism against Cuba. They then invited two important FBI officials to Havana. The United States has commented on this: "In June 1998, in the aftermath of a series of bombings and bomb threats against Cuban citizens and interests, a team from the FBI met in Havana with Cuban law enforcement authorities. The discussions focused on allegations that United States residents had participated in a terrorist conspiracy related to the bombings. At that time, Cuban officials shared evidence with the Federal Bureau of Investigation for analysis in Washington, D.C." To this day, despite significant proof, none of the 64 persons have been bothered by U.S. authorities.[304]

Three months later, on September 12, 1998, after careful investigation, the FBI arrested five Cuban agents who allegedly had infiltrated terrorists groups in Miami: René González Sehweret, Ramón Labañino Salazar, Fernando González Llort, Antonio Guerrero Rodriguez, and Gerardo Hernández Nordelo. On September 14, 1998, a Florida grand jury (public prosecutors office) accused the five of having infiltrated terrorist groups. The charge was legally untenable. The grand jury then changed its approach and advanced twenty-six federal charges. The first related to "a conspiracy to commit offenses against the United States" as agents of the Cuban government. The second charge referred to a conspiracy to "communicate information to Cuba relative to the national defense of the United States." The third charge accused Gerardo Hernández of quadruple homicide. According to the prosecution, he was directly responsible for the events of February 24, 1996, when two planes belonging to the terrorist organization Hermanos al Rescate (Brothers to the

Rescue) were shot down by Havana's air defense after having violated Cuban air space numerous times.[305]

During the trial, the prosecution was unable to present any proof in support of these three accusations, which were rejected by the defense. The other twenty-three charges were minor, referring to the use of false identity, having failed to register as agents of a foreign power, etc. The defense acknowledged these accusations, but invoked the Doctrine of Necessity, which states that the law may be ignored if the goal is to prevent a more serious offense. For example, breaking into a house to extinguish a fire is technically trespassing, but given that the objective is to prevent the house from burning, the law does not pursue the perpetrator. The defense admitted that the Five, from a technical point of view, had in fact violated the law, but explained the necessity for so doing: If the Five had revealed their true identities, they would have been unable to infiltrate the terrorist groups and thus could not have prevented attacks against Cuba.[306]

The prosecution, unable to prove acts of espionage, chose to accuse the Five of conspiracy to commit acts of espionage. Such accusations do not require proof. It is sufficient simply to convince the jurors that the accused are guilty "beyond a reasonable doubt."[307]

From their arrest until February 3, 2000, that is to say for 17 consecutive months, all five Cubans were held in solitary confinement, away from other inmates. They were denied external communication. This, despite the fact that the United States Penal Code states that isolation may be applied only to individuals who have committed blood crimes and then for a maximum duration of 60 days only.[308]

During the trial, the prosecution invoked the Classified Information Procedures Act (CIPA) and then presented the jury with documents to be used against the defendants. These documents were not shared with the defense, an action that prevented them from being challenged in court. Thus, 20,000 pages of documents were used against the defendants without the possibility of their being contested.[309]

Aware of the weakness of the charge and given the lack of factual proof, the prosecutor nonetheless repeated three times during the trial that the Five had come to Miami "to destroy the United States," something that failed to elicit a reaction from the court.[310]

The trial took place in Miami, a city hostile to the Havana government and controlled at all levels (city hall, police, the media, etc.) by the Cuban exile community, a situation that made an impartial verdict impossible. The court refused to move the trial to Fort Lauderdale, some 28 miles from Miami. This was a decision that violated the Sixth Amendment of the Constitution of the United States, which states that "the accused shall enjoy the right to a public and speedy trial by an impartial jury of the State and district wherein the crime shall have been committed." Judiciary legislation stipulates that the accused has the right to ask for a change of venue that would allow the trial to be moved to another city or district if the court considers that the place where the trial would normally be held is tainted by prejudice against the defendant. This ruling was not respected.[311]

Before the beginning of the trial, a vitriolic media campaign was launched against the Five. According to a poll commissioned by the defense and the court that was conducted in Miami-Dade County by psychologist Garry Morgan, 69 percent of the respondents were found to be prejudiced against the accused, and 49 percent admitted that they could not be fair and impartial if they were impaneled as members of the jury.[312]

El País ignores another key element in this case. Certain federal documents have revealed that numerous Miami journalists—44 in all—were paid by the U.S. government to publish negative articles concerning the Cuban Five. Their actions, in addition to being a serious breach of journalistic ethics, clearly influenced the jury. Thus, during the 194 days between the date of the arrests of the Five in September 1998 and their convictions in December 2001, the two principal Miami dailies, the *Miami Herald* and the *Nuevo Herald*—which is affiliated with *El País*—published a total of 1,111 articles, or an average of five per day—all hostile—dealing with the case of the Five.[313]

Several articles in the local press revealed that the jurors had been threatened with death were they to acquit the accused. According to an article in the *Nuevo Herald* of December 2, 2000, "*Miedo a ser jurado en juicio de espias*" (Fear of Being a Juror in the Spy Trial), "The fear of a violent reaction on the part of exiled Cubans if a jury decides to acquit the five men accused of being spies for the island regime has caused numerous potential candidates to request that the judge excuse them from their civic duty." One member of the jury testified: "Yes, I am afraid for my safety if the verdict does not satisfy the Cuban community."[314]

The transcript of the minutes of the trial also proves that the Five could not in any case expect to receive a just and impartial verdict. Judge Joan A. Leonard, who presided over the case, complained that the presence of cameramen and provocateurs in front of the courtroom doors intimidated the jurors—who, for example, were followed to their cars where their license plates were photographed. The members of the jury expressed these concerns to the judge who then drafted a report on the subject: "They are afraid because they feel themselves under pressure and because they are being filmed."[315]

The arguments demonstrating that the Five were innocent of espionage were not presented by the defense but rather by high-ranking U.S. military officers: U.S. Navy Rear Admiral Eugene Carroll, U.S. Army Major-General Edward Breed Atkeson, and U.S. Air Force Lieutenant General James R. Clapper. In order to justify the charge of "conspiracy to commit espionage," the prosecution relied on the fact that Antonio Guerrero worked in a metal workshop in the army training base at Boca Chica. The defense questioned the military officers:

> **Question for Admiral Eugene Carroll on Boca Chica:** "What information about the tactics and training of the U.S. Navy might be useful to the Cuban army?"
> **Response:** "None that I know of."

Questions to General Atkeson: "Are there differences in our relations with the Warsaw Pact and the Soviet Union in Europe and our relations with Cuba?"

"Yes, differences exist."

"What are these differences?"

"The Cubans do not represent a threat to us." [In so stating, Atkeson contradicted the prosecutor's claim that the Five "came to destroy the United States."]

"What is the relationship between the fear of being attacked and the gathering of information?"

"I think they use their intelligence services to discover if we are really preparing to attack them."

"In your examination of the documents, did you find any that were classified 'secret'?"

"No."

"Have you found any instructions to the agents to search for documents that could harm the United States?"

"No."

Questions to General Clapper: "Do you agree that access to public information does not constitute espionage?"

"Yes."

"Given your intelligence experience, do you feel that Cuba represents a military threat to the United States?"

"Not in the least. Cuba does not represent a threat."

"Did you find any proof that Gerardo Hernández was trying to get secret information?"

"As I recall, no."

"Instead, what you discovered was that he had asked someone to get publicly available information, right?"

"Yes."[316]

The FBI confirmed to the press that U.S. military secrets had never been put in danger. The Pentagon intervened and confirmed that it had no information indicating that the Five had access to information classified as either secret or sensitive.[317]

As for Hernández, who was accused of murder, the prosecution acknowledged that "in light of the evidence presented at trial, proving the involvement of Gerardo Hernández is an insurmountable obstacle for the United States."[318] The prosecution nonetheless insisted that the Hermanos al Rescate (Brothers to the Rescue) aircraft was shot down in international airspace, something that constitutes a serious crime. The release of satellite images in the possession of the United States would clarify this issue and indicate clearly whether the plane had been shot down in Cuban or international airspace. This in turn would either confirm or refute the guilt of Gerardo Hernández, accused of having informed Cuba of the aerial incursion. However, since 1996, Washington, invoking national security concerns, has refused to publish these images, even though the International Civil Aviation Organization, in charge of the investigation, has requested them on several occasions.[319]

According to *El País*, the role of the organization Hermanos al Rescate consisted of "distributing propaganda for democracy in Cuba and helping immigrants trying to reach the United States."[320] The Madrid daily said little else about it and discreetly avoided naming the leader of the organization, José Basulto, most likely because of his violent past. His background does not work in his favor and calls the paper's version of the facts squarely into question. Basulto has acknowledge having organized terrorist attacks against Cuba in the past. At no time was Basulto's name mentioned, even though he is still director of the organization.[321]

Despite the admission of the prosecutor, as well as a clear lack of evidence, all members of the jury, without having asked the accused or the prosecutor a single question, found Gerardo Hernández guilty of premeditated murder. The jurors had heard from a total of 74 witnesses, 43 of whom were witnesses for the prosecution, yet they did not ask for a single clarification. Despite a file that consisted of tens of thousands of pages, as well as several dozen charges, they announced in advance of their meetings the exact day and time they would render their verdict. They then deliberated only for a few hours. Ricardo Alarcón, former president of the Cuban Parliament, emphasized this anomaly: "You cannot announce a specific time when you will make your verdict public! This is an impossibility because no one can know how long such proceedings will last unless the case has been decided upon beforehand. This was, in addition, the longest trial in the history of U.S. justice."[322]

The Five were severely condemned. Gerardo Hernández Nordelo received two life sentences plus 15 years. Ramón Labañino Salazar was sentenced to life plus 18 years. Antonio Guerrero Rodriguez was sentenced to life plus 10 years. As for Fernando González Llort, he was sentenced to 19 years of prison, and René González Sehweret was sentenced to 15 years. In total, the Five received four life sentences plus 77 years of prison.[323]

By way of comparison, Antonio Guerrero, who did not have access to secret documents, was given the same life sentence as Robert Philip Hanssen, one of the most famous spies in the history of the United States, who for years stole thousands of secret documents that he sold to the Soviet Union and Russia.[324]

Similarly, *El País* did not see fit to quote the statement of Judge Joan A. Leonard regarding René González. Judge Leonard acknowledged that René González, sentenced to 15 years in prison for failing to register with the Department of State as an agent of a foreign nation, had indeed infiltrated violent groups in order to prevent future attacks against Cuba: "Terrorism, whether committed against innocent people in the United States or Cuba, Israel and Jordan, Northern Ireland or India, is malicious and evil, but the terrorist actions of others cannot excuse the wrong and illegal conduct of the accused or any other." In addition to condemning the Five to long prison sentences, the court took care to protect the violent groups in Florida linked to terrorism against Cuba. Indeed the prosecution had certain rather unusual things to say. In addition to the sentence of 15 years of imprisonment for René González, it also demanded an additional sanction of three years of supervised release afterward, expressing "concern that the accused, after having served his sentence, might resume his activities." The judge granted the motion and imposed yet another restriction on González: "As a special additional condition to his supervised release, the defendant is prohibited from associating with or visiting specific places where individuals or groups such as terrorists, members of organizations advocating violence, and organized crime figures are known to be or frequent." By doing so, Judge Leonard admitted the existence of such terrorist groups in Miami, without taking action against them.[325]

In 2003, the Cuban Five defense team filed the first federal appeal before the 11th Circuit Court of Appeals in Atlanta. On May 27, 2005, the United Nations Commission on Human Rights Working Group on Arbitrary Detentions declared the detention of the Five to be arbitrary and in violation of international law.[326]

On August 9, 2005, a three-judge panel of the 11th Circuit Court of Appeals in Atlanta overturned the convictions, having found that espionage and a threat to national security had not occurred. The Florida prosecution appealed the decision of the Atlanta Court of Appeals. For the first time in the history of U.S. jurisprudence, an appeals court decided to review its own judgment. Usually, a contested case goes on to the Supreme Court, but due to political pressures, the court agreed to rehear the two parties on February 14, 2006.[327]

On September 2, 2008, the Atlanta Court of Appeals upheld the sentences of Gerardo Hernández and René González, but invalidated the sentences of Antonio Guerrero, Fernando González, and Ramón Labañino. On this occasion, the court once again recognized that no secret document or information pertaining to national defense had been sent by the accused, thereby invalidating the charge of "conspiracy to commit espionage." Moreover, in a 16-page document, Phyllis Kravitch, one of three Court of Appeals judges, affirmed that the U.S. government had not provided evidence necessary to support the charge of "conspiracy to commit murder" levied against Gerardo Hernández.[328]

On June 15, 2009, the U.S. Supreme Court announced, without explanation, its decision not to consider the case of the Five, despite arguments provided by the defense team and twelve *amicus curiae* briefs. *Amicus curiae* (friends of the court) is a process that allows individuals, legal institutions, and legislatures to offer information on a case to the Supreme Court of the United States. This was the most important *amicus curiae* demand in the history of U.S. justice. Among these *amicus curiae* were ten Nobel Prize winners: José Ramos-Horta, Wole Soyinka, Adolfo Pérez Esquivel, Nadine Gordimer, Rigoberta Menchú, José Saramago, Zhores Alferov, Dario Fo, Günter Grass, and Mairead Corrigan Maguire. In the United States, the National Association of Criminal Defense Lawyers, the Cuban-American Scholars, the Ibero-American Federation of Ombudsmen, the National Jury Project, the William C. Velasquez Institute, the Mexican American Political Association, the National Lawyers Guild, the National Conference of Black Lawyers, the Howard University School of Law Civil Rights Clinic, the International Association of Democratic Lawyers, the Florida Association of Criminal Defense Lawyers Miami Chapter, the Center for International Policy, and the Council on Hemispheric Affairs also appealed to the Supreme Court. In addition, there were appeals from Mary Robinson, former president of Ireland and UN High Commissioner for Human Rights between 1997 and 2002; a unanimous Mexican Senate; the National Assembly of Panama; 75 members of the European Parliament; 56 Canadian and more than a hundred British parliamentarians, among others.[329]

On October 13, 2009, the U.S. District Court in Southern Florida, required by the Atlanta Court of Appeals to modify the prison terms for three of the Five, reviewed their sentences. Thus the life imprisonment plus 10 years of Antonio Guerrero was reduced to 21 years and 10 months, plus five years of supervised release. On December 8, 2009, Fernando González had his sentence reduced from 19 years to 17 years and nine months. As for Ramón Labañino, his penalty of life imprisonment plus 18 years was reduced to 30 years in prison.[330]

On June 14, 2010, the Five's defense team filed a writ of *habeas corpus* for Gerardo Hernández with the Miami Federal Court. This is the final legal recourse available within the U.S. judicial system. The appeal focused primarily on two points: first, no factual evidence had been provided to support the charge of "conspiracy to commit murder." Second, the accused did not receive a fair trial, because of the hostile atmosphere that reigned in Miami, especially because the U.S. government had paid local journalists to disseminate negative information about Cuba and the Five in the local media. To this day, the court has not rendered a decision.[331]

Several cases of psychological and mental torture have played out within the families of the Five. Adriana Pérez O'Connor, wife of Gerardo Hernández, has not been permitted to visit her husband since 1998. On June 25, 2002, after five years of waiting, she obtained a visa granting her the right to visit Hernández, who was held in Los Angeles. But upon her arrival in the United States, she was arrested by the FBI, interrogated for eleven hours, and then deported back to Cuba without having been allowed to see her husband. In order to complicate consular visits to the Five, the detainees were placed in penitentiaries spread across the United States.[332]

On October 7, 2011, René González was released from prison after completing his sentence. Sentenced to three years of probation because of his American citizenship, he remained in the United States. On May 3, 2013, Judge Leonard accepted his request to return to Cuba, provided he renounce his American citizenship, which he did.[333]

Wayne S. Smith, former U.S. ambassador to Cuba between 1979 and 1982, expressed his views on this matter. The U.S. diplomat was considerably more accurate and nuanced than *El País* about this case:

> The Five, Gerardo Hernandez, Luis Medina, Antonio Guerrero, Rene Gonzalez, and Ruben Campa, were members of the Cuban Intelligence Service to be sure. They had been sent to the United States, however, not to spy on the American government, its installations, or its personnel; rather they had been sent to penetrate Cuban exile organizations that were

carrying on terrorist activities against Cuba. The idea, then, once sufficient evidence of these activities had been gathered, was to invite representatives of the FBI to come to Cuba, and provide them with that evidence, in hopes that the U.S. would then take action to put a stop to such activities. In accordance with that plan, in June of 1998 three representatives of the FBI were invited to Cuba and met with their Cuban counterparts. They returned to the U.S. with 64 folders of information on exile activities. The Cubans then waited for the United States to take measures to halt terrorist actions. They waited in vain. No action whatsoever was taken. Rather, apparently able to determine from the evidence provided who had provided it, a few months later the FBI arrested the Cuban Five and, in 2001, they were submitted to a totally biased trial in Miami, where anti-Castro sentiment was so strong that, in effect, there was no chance of empanelling an impartial jury. . . .

In addition to the biased atmosphere in which the trial was held, prosecutors could present no evidence that the five had engaged in espionage or any other crime (other than being unregistered agents of a foreign power).[334]

El País has not seen fit to print the fact that this court case has been criticized from all sides. Colonel Lawrence Wilkerson, Chief of Staff to former Secretary of State Colin Powell (under the Bush administration), also spoke on this subject:

This case sort of takes the cake: to punish with life sentences men who came here to determine how and when their country was going to be attacked by people breaking U.S. law. These men were unarmed, not intent on any physical damage to the United States, and were motivated to protect their fellow citizens from invasion and repeated attacks by Cuban-Americans living in Florida.

And we have to ask also, just how is it that we have become a safe haven for alleged terrorists? How is it that we—the United

States of America—may rate a place on our own list of states
that sponsor terrorism?[335]

For the first time, the United Nations Commission on Human
Rights condemned the trial in the United States, noting that "the
biased and prejudicial atmosphere against the accused" made it
impossible for a Miami court to demonstrate the "objectivity and
impartiality that is required in order to conform to the standards
of a fair trial." Amnesty International also considers that the five
Cubans failed to receive a fair trial.[336]

The case of the Cuban Five illustrates the double standard that
the United States applies in its "war on terrorism." This double
standard appears to be applied equally by Western media that not
only continue to censor this judicial and political scandal, but also
to ignore the history of terrorism against Cuba. Furthermore, in
their coverage they absolve Luis Posada Carriles, the most dan-
gerous terrorist in the Western Hemisphere according to the FBI,
by refusing to name him as the terrorist that he is. Other terms
are preferred, such as "militant," "Cuban militant," "anti-Castro
militant," "Cuban exile," "anti-Castro exile," "militant anticom-
munist," and simply "anti." Western media also accept, assimilate,
and promote the doctrine, elaborated by Washington, that dis-
tinguishes between "good" and "bad" terrorists. In so doing, they
tacitly justify violence and fail to denounce what they call arbitrary terrorism. Their wording varies with the intended victim.
If the victim is Western—more specifically, if he or she is from a
developed country—those responsible are qualified as hardened
criminals who fear neither God nor law. When the victim is from
the third world, Cuba for example, the perpetrators become "militants," "Cuban militants," "anti-Castro militants," "Cuban exiles,"
"anti-Castro exiles," "militant anti-" or again simply "anti."[337]

In terms of the case of the Cuban Five, *El País* has issued erroneous statements, obscured many facts, and censored the historical
context. The Spanish newspaper has not deigned to cross-check
information and has accepted, hook, line, and sinker, the U.S.

government's version of events despite the existence of many facts and the testimonies of eminent personalities, all of which contradict the official thesis.

8

The Case of Alan Gross

EL PAÍS HAS ALSO addressed the case of Alan Gross, a U.S. citizen employed by Alternative Development, Inc. (DAI), a subcontractor of the U.S. Agency for International Development (USAID), which itself is an entity of the Department of State. Gross was sentenced to 15 years in prison in Cuba for espionage and internal subversion after, according to Cuban authorities, entering the island with highly sophisticated satellite equipment to be distributed to the internal opposition.

El País correspondent Mauricio Vicent underscores that according to Washington, Gross "went to Cuba to help the small Jewish community and provide its members with various equipment for connecting to the Internet." Unlike the Cuban declarations, the journalist takes no typographical precautions (quotation marks) when it comes to describing the position of the United States.[338]

Gross is considered by the Madrid daily to be legitimate. Vicent does not provide additional information, and he has not seen fit to visit the Jewish community in Havana to corroborate the United States's point of view.

Other journalists, doubtless more prudent, have made this approach and offer a completely different perspective. The official version of the United States and the Gross family is contradicted by the Jewish community in Havana itself. Its representatives claim not to know Alan Gross and never to have met him despite his five trips to Cuba in 2009. Adela Dworin, president of the Beth Shalom Temple, rejects Washington's claims: "It's harmful. . . . The saddest part is that they tried to involve the Jewish community in Cuba, which has nothing to do with this." For her part, Mayra Levy, speaker of the Sephardic Hebraic Center, declared that she did not know who Gross was and added that he had never been to her institution. For its part, the Associated Press reported that "the leaders of the Cuban Jewish community have denied that the American contractor Alan Gross . . . had collaborated with them."[339] Similarly, the Jewish Telegraphic Agency stated that "the main Jewish groups in Cuba have denied having had any contract with Alan Gross or any knowledge of his project."[340]

Reverend Odén Marichal, secretary of the Consejo de Iglesias de Cuba (Cuban Council of Churches, or CIC), which includes the non-Catholic Christian religious institutions and the Jewish community in Cuba, confirmed this position at a meeting with Peter Brennan, State Department Coordinator for Cuban Affairs. On the occasion of the General Assembly of the Churches of Christ in the United States, held in Washington in November 2010, the religious leader rejected Gross's allegations. "What we made clear is what the Jewish community, a member of the Council of Churches of Cuba, told us: 'We never had a relationship with that gentleman; he never brought us any equipment.' They denied any kind of relationship with Alan Gross."[341]

Secretary of State Hillary Clinton tried to mobilize the Jewish community of the United States in favor of Gross: "I am really making an appeal to the active Jewish community here in our country to join in this cause." But the efforts of the Secretary of State found little echo among U.S. Jewish leaders.[342]

Arturo Lopez-Levy, Secretary of B'nai B'rith in the Cuban Jewish community between 1999 and 2001 and currently a professor at the University of Denver, is also skeptical of the U.S. version of Gross's activities in Cuba:

Gross was not arrested because he is Jewish, nor is it likely that he was detained because of his alleged activities in helping the Cuban Jewish community with technology, which already had a computer lab, email, and access to the Internet before he arrived in Havana on his several visits. . . . [The Jews of Cuba do not] gather in the synagogue to conspire with the political opposition, because that would jeopardize the cooperation with the government that is necessary for activities such as the emigration to Israel program, the Birthright Project, by which young Cuban Jews travel to Israel every year, or to process humanitarian aid. To protect what matters most, they keep themselves as far as possible from misconceived U.S. political interventions in Cuba's internal affairs. Gross did not come to Cuba to work for a Jewish organization, but rather to work for the USAID.[343]

Former U.S. ambassador Wayne S. Smith notes that Gross "was involved in a program which clearly had hostile intentions toward Cuba because the intention was nothing less than regime change."[344]

This view is shared by Robert Pastor, former national security adviser for Latin America under U.S. President Jimmy Carter: "Of course, this is covert work. It's about regime change."[345]

Indeed, as revealed in an investigation conducted by the Associated Press, Alan Gross was aware of the illegal nature of his activities and the risks involved, and the reasons for which his compensation amounted to half a million dollars. In his reports to his superiors, he acknowledged that it was "a very risky business." He wrote: "We're playing with fire, and the detection of satellite signals would be catastrophic." The Associated Press notes that "the reports indicate that he knew his activities were illegal in Cuba and he was worried about the danger he was running." Among electronic equipment smuggled to Cuba was "a special mobile phone chip, which according to experts, is frequently used by the Pentagon and the CIA to render satellite signals virtually undetectable." The Associated Press adds: "These chips are usually provided to the Department of Defense and the CIA." For its part, the State Department has acknowledged "the risk run" by Alan Gross in Cuba.[346]

In the case of Alan Gross, *El País* has once again obscured the facts and accepted unconditionally the U.S. government's official version, although many concordant sources undermine the position advanced by Washington. On this subject as well, balance, the plurality of views, and nuance are absent from the debate.

9

Cuban Emigration to the United States

IN AN ARTICLE IN its October 9, 2011 edition, *El País* invokes the Cuban migration issue, suggesting that the number of Cubans attempting to reach the United States is steadily increasing.[347] Citing the English-language Florida daily the *Miami Herald*, the Madrid newspaper notes that U.S. Department of Homeland Security statistics show a net increase in Cuban migration to the North.

According to *El País*, this massive emigration of Cubans is due to "a worsening of the economic situation and increased social malaise on the island." Thus, a Cuban migration boom illustrates the failure of the socioeconomic system in place in Cuba since 1959, a system unable to meet the needs of the population, a substantial proportion of which opts for sunnier climes.

The information provided by *El País* is incomplete in a number of respects. The newspaper does not, for example, cite pre-1959 Cuban migration statistics. It also fails to mention two unique key factors related to Cuba, the goals of which are to encourage emigration, namely the Cuban Adjustment Act and economic sanctions against the island. Furthermore, it provides no information on migration statistics in other Latin American nations, statistics that would allow for a comparative study to determine whether Cuban migration issues are in fact unique to that country.

It is indeed curious that *El País* makes no reference to pre-Revolution Cuban migratory activity, even though statistics are available from 1820 to 2010.[348] These statistics make it relatively easy to compare the level of migration before the triumph of the Cuban Revolution with the present, something that allows us to assess the impact of the revolutionary process on migratory trends.

From 1940 to 1949, Cuba, with 25,976 departures, had significantly surpassed the number of emigrants of the prior decade. This is a figure greater than that of the total migration from all Caribbean nations (20,218). Cuban emigration had also surpassed significantly that of all Central American nations (20,135) and the whole of South America (19,662). Even when they are included, the figures from Africa (6,720) and Oceania (1,262) did not reach that of the Caribbean island.[349]

From 1950 to 1959, the Cuban migratory impulse climbed to 73,221 departures, three times higher than that of the previous decade. Cuba outstripped its Caribbean neighbors as well as the total of all emigrants from this region (42,440), a figure that remained significantly lower than that of the "Pearl of the Antilles." The whole of Central America followed far behind with 40,201 departures. In terms of South America, no country in this region registered more emigrants than Cuba, neither Argentina (16,346), Colombia (15,567), nor Brazil (11,547), which were the nations with the highest migration propensity. Cuba easily outperformed other South American countries, whose departures, when taken together, totaled 34,858.[350]

In addition, Cuba produced a much larger exodus than that of Africa (13,016) and Oceania (11,353) and met and exceeded that of many Asian population giants such as China (8,836), India (1,850), Iran (3,195), and Turkey (2,980).[351]

Many European countries did not reach the Cuban emigration rates during this decade. Hungary, with 31,661 departures for the United States, and Belgium, with 18,885, did not surpass Cuba in terms of migration. Cuba counted exactly 45 times more emigrants than Czechoslovakia (1,624), and more than Denmark (10,918) and France (50,113) taken together.

Cuba also far exceeded Greece (45,153), Ireland (47,189), the Netherlands (46,703), Norway (22,806), and Sweden (21,418). It saw more emigration than Spain (6,880), Switzerland (17,577), and Yugoslavia (8,966) combined. The Caribbean island counted five times more emigrants than Portugal (13,928), 11 times more than Poland (6465), 80 times more than Romania (914), and 161 times more than the Soviet Union (453).[352]

Compared to Asia, Cuba had more emigrants than Japan (40,651), Israel (21,376), the Philippines (17,245), Hong Kong (13,781), China (8,836), Korea (4,845), Turkey (2,980), Iran (3195), India (1,850), and Vietnam (290).[353]

In 1959, Cuba ranked second in America in terms of migration to the United States, behind only Mexico (273,847), and produced nearly twice as many immigrants as Central America (40,201) and a figure equivalent to that of the whole of South America (78,418).[354]

In addition, since November 2, 1966, the Cuban Adjustment Act, passed by the U.S. Congress, has been in force. It is unique in the world in that it has as its goals encouraging illegal emigration and politicizing the migration issue in the country's ideological war against Havana. It allows any Cuban emigrant to the United States who arrives either legally or illegally, peacefully or by force, on or after January 1, 1959, to automatically obtain, after one year in the country, permanent residence status and many other benefits in terms of employment and housing.[355]

Ricardo Alarcón, president of the Cuban Parliament, highlighted the unique nature of the Cuban Adjustment Act:

> There are two key elements in this legislation. Firstly, it refers to a very specific date, and everyone knows what that evokes. What exactly does it mean that people who left after that date

are accepted? It means, of course, that all those who arrived earlier are excluded, and we're talking about the country that at that time accounted for the second largest number of emigrants to the United States. This law does not apply to those who arrived before January 1, 1959, and they cannot therefore benefit from it.

Why are people of Cuban origin who arrived in the United States before that date excluded? Simply because they represent a very large population, otherwise there would be no reason to set a date.

[Furthermore] this law has a destabilizing effect because it is the instrument of a policy that seeks to promote the emigration of Cubans to the United States. The only category of people among all the inhabitants of the planet who are granted the privilege of acquiring legal residence in the United States, by simply presenting themselves to the authorities, are those of Cuban origin.

The United States is the only country in the world to have such a law, one that stimulates and, through publicity and media campaigns as well as other forms of enticement, encourages Cubans to emigrate—but only Cubans. There are other incentives and assistance programs, such as the Cuban Refugee Program, where housing and jobs are provided to immigrants, contrary to what is available to other immigrants who, in general, are abandoned to their fate once they achieve legal status and are imprisoned when they find themselves in trouble. Clearly, they do not enjoy these privileges.[356]

In addition to the Cuban Adjustment Act, an objective vector designed to incite legal and illegal migration, factor in that the economic sanctions imposed since 1960 also stimulate emigration to the United States. These sanctions affect the daily lives of Cuban people, and the most vulnerable groups sometimes choose to leave the country. This parameter must be taken into account in any analysis of the Cuban migration issue.

Given these facts, it would not be incongruous to think that in 2010, Cuba ranked first on the continent in terms of emigration. But this is not the case. Despite its pre-Revolution ranking, the Cuban Adjustment Act of 1966, and economic sanctions, the island has seen only 33,372 departures, compared to 53,890 for the Dominican Republic and 138,717 for Mexico. Thus Cuba (population 11.2 million) lost its second place position to the Dominican Republic, which has a smaller population (9.8 million people), no Adjustment Act, and is not subjected to economic sanctions. Other Latin American nations also saw significant emigration, for example, Haiti (22,336 of a population of 9.9 million), Jamaica (19,439 of 2.8 million), and El Salvador (18,547 of 7 million).[357]

Similarly, under the Cuban Adjustment Act of 1966, there is not a single Cuban national who is unlawfully present in the United States. Cuba is the only nation in the world to have no illegal nationals in the United States. In terms of official figures for other countries, it is well to note that the number of immigrants unlawfully present in the United States on January 1, 2010 rose to 10.8 million, according to the U.S. Immigration Services.[358]

CUBAN MIGRATION REFORM

Regarding the migration reform that came into force on January 14, 2013, *El País* reports that Cubans can now travel abroad "after being barred for years" from doing so by the authorities.[359] Again, the reality is somewhat different, and the facts are there to prove it.

Long awaited and responding to popular demand, this reform facilitates foreign travel for Cubans. They no longer need the famous Carta Blanca (white card), issued by the authorities for the sum of $150, nor will it be necessary to obtain a "letter of invitation," at a cost of $200, from a foreigner to leave the country.[360]

Now, in order to travel abroad, Cubans need only a passport (valid for six years) at a price of 100 convertible pesos (80 euros), a host country visa, and the financial resources necessary to allow them to discover the world for two years without further formality, compared to eleven months before. Beyond this 24-month period, those wishing to extend their stay outside national territory may apply to do so at the local consulate. They may also return to Cuba and leave for another trip of similar duration, something that is renewable indefinitely.[361]

Contrary to popular belief, the need for permission to leave the country was not instituted by the revolutionary government in 1959. Max Lesnik, director of Radio Miami, recalled that it dates from 1954 and was imposed by the military regime of Fulgencio Batista. This arrangement was maintained when Fidel Castro came to power in order to limit, among other things, the brain drain to the United States.[362]

Since the triumph of the Revolution, the United States has used the issue of migration as a tool to destabilize Cuba, at first welcoming war criminals and corrupt officials of the former regime, and later by encouraging a brain drain, aimed primarily at doctors.[363] In this regard, highly qualified candidates for emigration are required to obtain permission from the immigration authorities. Decree-Law 302 provides for such restrictions in order to "preserve a skilled workforce for the economic, social and scientific-technical development of the country, as well as for the safety and protection of official information."[364]

Doctors are of particular concern. Since 2006, the Cuban Medical Program (CMPP), established by the Bush administration and continued by Barack Obama, aims to encourage Cuban doctors on missions abroad to abandon their posts by offering them the prospect of practicing in the United States, thereby depriving the Cuban nation of valuable human capital.[365] To date, several hundred Cuban doctors, particularly those serving in Venezuela, have allowed themselves to be tempted by the offer.[366]

This policy is part of the economic war that the United States has been waging against Cuba since 1960. The imposition of extremely harsh sanctions, sanctions that are contrary to international law because they are both retroactive and extraterritorial, affect all segments of Cuban society, especially the most vulnerable. The medical services provided by Cuban doctors outside national borders are the primary source of income for the nation, generating more revenue than tourism, money transfers from the Cuban community abroad, or the production of nickel.[367]

As for the United States, the State Department did not fail to criticize the restrictions, among others, imposed upon health care professionals in order to counter U.S. policy aimed at depriving Cuba of highly valued professionals, all in the name of a conflict between the two nations that has raged for more than half a century. Victoria Nuland, a U.S. diplomatic spokesperson, has addressed this issue: "We must recall that the Cuban government has not lifted the measures currently in force to preserve what it calls 'human capital' created by the revolution."[368]

Similarly, Nuland said that the immigration policy of the United States toward Cuba would not be changed and that the Cuban Adjustment Act would be maintained, and at the same time called on Cubans "not to risk their lives"[369] by illegally crossing the Straits of Florida.

Nuland's statement does not escape certain contradictions. Instead of granting a visa to any candidate for emigration, something fully in line with the philosophy of the Cuban Adjustment Act, the United States limits their number to 20,000 per year, in accordance with agreements signed with Havana in 1994.[370] Meanwhile, Washington refuses to repeal the Cuban Adjustment Act, a law that allows Cubans to settle permanently in the United States without requiring them to obtain a visa.

The reform of the migration policy provides Cubans greater freedom to travel abroad, even if, and contrary to the assertions of *El País*, between the year 2000 and August 31, 2012, of a total of 941,953 applications to leave the country, 99.4 percent were granted permission. Only 0.6 percent of those applying were denied. Moreover, there is no particular proclivity on the part of Cubans to emigrate. The vast majority who travel abroad choose to return home. Of the 941,953 people who left the country between

2000 and 2012, only 12.8 percent chose to settle abroad, compared to 87.2 percent who returned to Cuba.[371]

Moreover, it will now be easier for Cubans to return to their country of origin. Indeed, the entry permit—adopted in 1961 for reasons of national security at a time when Cuban exiles under the control of the CIA were committing acts of terrorism and sabotage on the island and when the vast majority of the candidates for departure were motivated by political reasons—will no longer be required.[372]

Most Cubans now living abroad are no longer hostile exiles but rather economic migrants who aspire to normal and peaceful relationships with their country of origin. They may return to the island as many times as they wish, as was the case before, but now they may do so without the need for redundant paperwork. Moreover, the only class of Cubans who had not been allowed to return to their country of origin were the so-called *balseros* (boat people). Although they left the country in the early 1990s during the "Special Period" that followed the dissolution of the Soviet Union, a time marked by economic hardship in Cuba and renewed hostility from the United States, they may now return to the island. It is the same for doctors and elite athletes who chose to leave the country during a stay abroad. The last administrative obstacles preventing the return of these emigrants were lifted in January 2013.[373]

Migration reform responds to the national aspirations of Cubans, many of whom wish simply to migrate abroad temporarily, raise funds, and return to Cuba to establish a small business. Each year since 2010, nearly 1,000 Cubans living abroad choose to return home and settle permanently on the island. The new immigration policy eliminates unnecessary bureaucratic obstacles and helps to normalize relations between the Cuban nation and its emigrant population.[374]

These facts concerning migration have not caught the attention of *El País*. The paper provides no explanation for its focus on Cuba when, for example, the Dominican Republic has a higher level of emigration, a population smaller than that of Cuba, and no law of adjustment, and is not subjected to economic sanctions. On this theme, *El País* begins with an incorrect assumption, one that is contradicted by the facts on the ground and statistical reality, something that leads inevitably to logically erroneous conclusions.

Conclusion

AN ANALYSIS OF THE media coverage of Cuban life by the Spanish daily *El País* is revealing in several respects. First, analysis undermines the editorial board's claims of impartiality. Its journalistic coverage is singularly lacking in diversity, balance, and nuance. It publishes information that is regularly truncated, often incomplete, and systematically negative—the censorship, for example, of any information that paints a picture of Cuba that is even slightly positive. This casts a shadow over the credibility and the professionalism of *El País*. The paper appears to defend and follow a specific political agenda, rather than presenting its readers with a broad overview of Cuban reality.

On certain subjects, *El País* conceals a wide range of evidence, omissions that inevitably create errors in public opinion regarding daily life in Cuba, human rights, Yoani Sánchez, and migration. In other cases, the newspaper does not hesitate to spread, quite incomprehensibly, falsehoods that do not stand up under analysis; for example, anything that touches upon Cuban social achievements. On still other aspects—internal opposition, for example—*El País* is quite verbose, yet at the same time conceals fundamental facts, namely funding by the United States. At other times—the case of the Cuban Five—the newspaper prefers to maintain a hermetic silence about the reasons for the Five's presence in Miami. In doing so, *El País* is completely at variance with journalistic ethics that prohibit "the intention to defame," "factual distortion," and "lies, manipulation, censorship and self-censorship."

In light of the position taken by *El País*, it is hardly surprising to discover that in a confidential memorandum sent to the State Department, the U.S. Interests Section in Havana is quite pleased with the editorial line of the Spanish newspaper of reference. The U.S. diplomats are fulsome in their praise of Mauricio Vicent, the paper's Havana correspondent, with whom they maintain close contact. Vicent "is generally considered among the very best, if not the best informed foreign correspondent in town. Vicent is well known to the USINT," a cable abbreviation for the U.S. Interests Section in Havana, and has met regularly with U.S. diplomats, the memorandum states.[375]

Similarly, another memorandum issued by the U.S. Embassy in Madrid and made public by WikiLeaks revealed that in April 2008, Juan Luís Cebrián, CEO of the Grupo PRISA, the owner of *El País*, had met secretly in Madrid with Thomas Shannon, Assistant Secretary of State for Western Hemisphere Affairs under the Bush administration, to explore issues concerning Latin America, especially Cuba, Venezuela, Argentina, Mexico, and Colombia. *El País* has never revealed the content of this meeting to its readership.[376]

Is the position of *El País* toward Cuba—and more generally, that of the Western media—surprising when we understand its collusion with powerful moneyed interests? One has reason to doubt it. A country that has the audacity to attempt to build a society based on sharing and solidarity and to erect a social republic in which basic human interest prevails, despite—it must be recognized—its imperfect character, its internal contradictions, and mistakes, will only be vilified by the defenders of the established order, particularly in a period when the dominant ideology glorifies accumulation and individualism. Victor Hugo said, "History has always courted the powerful." In reality, the media's role is to teach the public respect for social hierarchies and economic interests, to convince them of the legitimacy of established privileges and the worthiness of the propertied classes.

Back in 1880, at a time when media monopolies were not yet a confirmed reality, John Swinton, then editor of the *New York Times*, had some reservations about the freedom of the press when it clashed with government policy. On the occasion of a reception organized in his honor, a member of the assembly proposed a toast to freedom of the press. Swinton then made the following statement:

> An independent press does not exist, either in America or in the world. You know it and I know it. There is not one among you who would dare to publish his true opinions, and if he did, you know in advance that they would never be printed. I am paid weekly to keep my true opinions out of the newspaper for which I work. Others of you are paid the same amount for similar work, and anyone who would be stupid enough to publish an honest opinion would be on the street immediately looking for a new job. If I authorized the publication of a truthful opinion in a single edition of my newspaper, I would lose my job in less than 24 hours. The function of the journalist is to destroy the truth, to lie radically, to pervert, to vilify, to grovel at the feet of the elite and sell himself, sell his country and his race for his daily bread, or what amounts to the same, his salary. You know it and I know it. How stupid it is to raise a toast to the independent press. We are the tools and vassals of rich men who control from behind the scenes. We are their puppets, they pull the strings and we dance to their tune. Our talents, our potential, and our lives are the property of these men. We are prostitutes of the intellect.[377]

Swinton's judgment, unquestionably severe, reflects a reality more important today than ever. Freedom and the duty to inform are by definition pitted against economic and financial power in an unequal battle in which truth is often the first casualty. A free and independent press must remain free and independent, not only from political but also from economic power, so that it can play its proper role in a democracy.

It is, nonetheless, difficult to continually mislead public opinion. On September 9, 1656, French philosopher and theologian Blaise Pascal, in the midst of a debate with the Jesuits, sent a letter that can be found in his work *Les Provinciales* (Provincial letters), denouncing their willingness to obscure reality. He expressed the following thought: "It is a strange and long war, the one in which violence attempts to suppress truth. Yet for all its efforts, violence can never weaken truth, but only serve to raise it higher." Pascal concludes with this warning: "Truth endures forever and in the end triumphs over its enemies, because truth is eternal and powerful."

Notes

1. Included in Florida's *El Nuevo Herald*.
2. The Grupo PRISA, whose main shareholder is Liberty Acquisition Holdings of U.S. investors Nicolas Berggruen and Martin E. Franklin, also owns Cadena SER, Cinco Días, Grupo Santillana, Alfaguara, Taurus, Aguilar, Diario AS, Los 40 Main, Maxima FM, M80 Radio Radiolé, Cadena Dial, PRISA TV, Localia, and Digital Plus, among others.
3. Grupo PRISA, "Quiénes somos," http://www.PRISA.com/quienes-somos/.
4. Syndicat national des journalistes, "Charte d'éthique professionnelle des journalistes," March 2011, http://www.snj.fr/spip.php?article1032.
5. *Manuel de estilo del diario* El País, Título 1: Principios, Sección 1: Política editorial, 1.2.
6. Ibid., 1.3.
7. Ibid., 1.12.
8. Ibid., 2.44.
9. EFE, "Cuba expulsa a corresponsal de *El País*," September 4, 2011.
10. "El régimen cubano retira a acreditación al corresponsal de *El País* en La Habana," *El País*, September 4, 2011; conversation with Max Lesnik, director of *Radio Miami*, September 13, 2011.
11. "El régimen cubano retira a acreditación al corresponsal de *El País* en La Habana."

12. *Cubainformación*, "Conferencia de Carlos Tena," October 20, 2011, http://www.youtube.com/watch?v=mWN0KScEUXo&feature=pla yer_embedded.
13. Correspondence between Gustave Flaubert and George Sand, September 8, 1871.
14. Associated Press, "El País va por mercado hispano en EU," March 8, 2011.
15. "Vuelve el Che," *El País*, July 17, 1997; Pascual Serrano, "El Che y los editoriales de El País, una comparación entre hace diez años y ahora," *Rebelión*, October 12, 2007.
16. "Caudillo Guevara," *El País*, October 10, 2007.
17. "Orden de callar," *El País*, September 6, 2011.
18. Ibid.
19. Raúl Castro Ruz, "Discurso pronunciado por el General de Ejército Raúl Castro Ruz, Presidente de los Consejos de Estado y de Ministros, en la clausura del Sexto Período Ordinario de Sesiones de la Séptima Legislatura de la Asamblea Nacional del Poder Popular, en el Palacio de Convenciones, el 18 de diciembre de 2010, Año 52 de la Revolución," *República de Cuba*, December 18, 2010, http://www.cuba.cu/gobierno/Raúldiscursos/2010/esp/r181210e.html.
20. Raúl Castro Ruz, "Intervención del General de Ejército Raúl Castro Ruz, Presidente de los Consejos de Estado y de Ministros de la República de Cuba en la Clausura del X Periodo de Sesiones de la Séptima Legislatura de la Asamblea Nacional del Poder Popular," December 13, 2012, http://www.cubadebate.cu/Raúl-castro-ruz/2012/12/13/Raúl-todo-lo-que-hagamos-va-dirigido-a-la-preservacion-y-desarrollo-en-cuba-de-una-sociedad-socialista-sustentable-y-prospera-fotos/.
21. Raúl Castro Ruz, "Discurso pronunciado por el General de Ejército Raúl Castro Ruz."
22. Raúl Castro, "Toda resistencia burocrática al estricto cumplimiento de los acuerdos del Congreso, respaldados masivamente por el pueblo, será inútil," *CubaDebate*, August 1, 2011.
23. Raúl Castro, "Discurso pronunciado por el General de Ejército Raúl Castro Ruz."
24. Fidel Castro Ruz, "Discurso pronunciado por Fidel Castro Ruz, Presidente de la República de Cuba, en el acto por el aniversario 60 de su ingreso a la universidad, efectuado en el Aula Magna de la Universidad de La Habana," November 17, 2005, http://www.cuba.cu/gobierno/discursos/2005/esp/f171105e.html.

25. Raúl Castro, "Discurso pronunciado por el General de Ejército Raúl Castro Ruz."
26. Ibid.
27. Raúl Castro, "Toda resistencia burocrática al estricto cumplimiento de los acuerdos del Congreso."
28. Raúl Castro, "Texto íntegro del Informe Central al VI Congreso del PCC," April 16, 2011, http://www.cubadebate.cu/opinion/2011/04/16/texto-integro-del-informe-central-al-vi-congreso-del-pcc/.
29. Raúl Castro, "Toda resistencia burocrática al estricto cumplimiento de los acuerdos del Congreso, respaldados masivamente por el pueblo, será inútil," *CubaDebate*, August 1, 2011.
30. Raúl Castro, "Toda resistencia burocrática al estricto cumplimiento de los acuerdos del Congreso."
31. Raúl Castro, "Discurso pronunciado por el General de Ejército Raúl Castro Ruz."
32. Partido Comunista de Cuba, "Resolución sobre los lineamientos de la política económica y social del partido y la Revolución" April 18, 2011.
33. Raúl Castro, "Informe central al VI Congreso del Partido Comunista de Cuba," April 16, 2011, http://www.cuba.cu/gobierno/Raúldiscursos/2011/esp/r160411e.html.
34. Ibid.
35. Félix López, "Burocratismo, de regla a excepción," *Granma*, January 29, 2011; EFE, "Diario oficial arremete contra burócratas," January 29, 2011.
36. José Alejandro Rodríguez, "Menos respuestas cuando más se necesitan," *Juventud Rebelde*, July 6, 2011.
37. Agence France Presse, "Figura histórica del castrismo aplaude la "desestatización," November 23, 2010.
38. Agence France Presse, "Transición del 'disparate' al socialismo, dice Guevara," June 24, 2011.
39. Agence France Presse, "Figura histórica del castrismo aplaude la desestatización."
40. Raúl Castro, "Informe central al VI Congreso del Partido Comunista de Cuba," April 16, 2011.
41. Raúl Castro, "Discurso pronunciado por el Primer Secretario del Comité Central del Partido, Raúl Castro Ruz, en la clausura del VI Congreso del Partido Comunista de Cuba, en el Palacio de Convenciones," April 19, 2011, http://www.cuba.cu/gobierno/Raúldiscursos/2011/esp/r190411e.html.

42. Salim Lamrani, *État de siège: Les sanctions économiques des États-Unis contre Cuba* (Paris: Editions Estrella, 2011).
43. Ibid.
44. Ibid.
45. *El País*, "Salir de Cuba," January 15, 2013.
46. Ibid.
47. Mick Hillyard and Vaughne Miller, "Cuba and the Helms-Burton Act," House of Commons Research Paper 98/114, December 14, 1998, 8. See also the statistics of the Central Intelligence Agency, "The World Factbook: Cuba," January 7, 2013, https://www.cia.gov/library/publications/the-world-factbook/geos/cu.html.
48. UNESCO, Latin American Laboratory for Evaluation and Quality of Education, "Learning in Latin America," September 3, 1999.
49. Margarita Barrio, "Obtuvo Cuba las más altas calificaciones de la calidad de la educación," *Juventud Rebelde*, June 21, 2008, http://www.juventudrebelde.cu/cuba/2008-06-21/obtuvo-cuba-las-mas-altas-calificaciones-en-evaluacion-de-la-calidad-de-la-educacion/.
50. UNESCO, "La crise cachée: Les conflits armés et l'éducation," Rapport mondial 2011 (Paris: Nations Unies, 2011), 95, http://unesdoc.unesco.org/images/0019/001917/191794f.pdf.
51. Alejandra Agudo, "La Unesco alerta de la condena al paro de los españoles sin formación," *El País*, September 16, 2012.
52. UNESCO, "Informe de 2012: Los jóvenes y las competencias: Trabajar con la educación," 2012, 370, http://www.unesco.org/new/es/education/themes/leading-the-international-agenda/efareport/reports/2012-skills/.
53. Ibid., 180.
54. Ministère de l'education nationale, "L'éducation nationale en chiffres," *République française*, 2012, http://www.education.gouv.fr/cid57111/l-education-nationale-en-chiffres.html.
55. *Opera Mundi*, "Cuba registra menor taxa de mortalidade infantil das Américas," January 3, 2013, http://operamundi.uol.com.br/conteudo/noticias/26374/cuba+registra+menor+taxa+de+mortalidade+infantil+das+americas+.shtml.
56. "Cuba: Centenaires grâce au système," *Le Figaro*, May 22, 2009.
57. Commission Economique Pour l'Amérique Latine (CEPAL), *Indicadores del desarrollo socioeconómico de América Latina* (Paris: Nations Unies, 2002), 12, 13, 39, 41, 43–47, 49–56, 66–67, 716–33.

58. American Association for World Health, "Denial of Food and Medicine: Impact of the U.S. Embargo on Health and Nutrition in Cuba," March 1997.

59. Diane Kuntz, "Statement from American Public Health Association," American Public Health Association, May 2, 1996.

60. Edward W. Campion and Stephen Morrissey, "A Different Model: Medical Care in Cuba," *New England Journal of Medecine*, January 24, 2013, 297–99.

61. Ibid.

62. Alberto Pérez, "La ONU y la Universidad de Harvard elogian el Sistema Cubano de Salud," *Granma*, April 5, 2005.

63. O. Fonticoba Gener, "Mantiene Cuba alto índice de desarrollo humano," *Granma*, October 1, 2011.

64. Orfilio Peláez and Rafael Pérez Valdés, "Más de 76 000 jóvenes estudian en las facultades de Medicina y otras dependencias," *Granma*, May 6, 2005.

65. "Director regional de OIT califica de 'casi un milagro' sistema cubano de seguridad social," *Granma*, March 30, 2005.

66. AIN, "Cuba, 4,7 de mortalidad infantil, la más baja de su historia," January 2, 2009; José A. de la Osa, "¡4,7!" *Granma*, January 2, 2008.

67. José A. de la Osa, Cuba es ejemplo en la protección a la infancia," *Granma*, April 12, 2008.

68. Fernando Ravsberg, "UNICEF: Cuba sin desnutrición infantil," BBC, January 26, 2010.

69. Radio Havane Cuba, "L'UNICEF signale que Cuba est un exemple en matière des droits de l'homme," June 1, 2012.

70. *Cubainformación*, "Entrevista a representante de UNICEF en Cuba," June 4, 2012, http://www.cubainformacion.tv/index.php?option =com_content&task=view&id=43657&Itemid=86.

71. Lisandra Fariña Acosta, "Ce pays est un laboratoire de développement social," *Granma*, June 7, 2012.

72. Marcos Alfonso, "Cuba: Ejemplo de la protección de la infancia, reconoce UNICEF," AIN, July 18, 2010.

73. UNICEF, *Progreso para la infancia: Un balance sobre la nutrición*, 2011.

74. Alvaro de Cózar, "146 millones de niños sufren hambre: UNICEF denuncia que el porcentaje de niños desnutridos es prácticamente el mismo desde hace 15 años," *El País*, May 3, 2006.

75. Save the Children, "Informe Estado Mundial de las madres 2011," 2012, http://www.savethechildren.es/ver_doc.php?id=115.

76. *CubaDebate*, "Cuba presenta exitosas vacunas contra el cáncer," September 25, 2012; Marie-France Cros, "Pourquoi se faire soigner à Cuba?" *La Libre*, January 10, 2013.

77. "Cuba presenta la primera vacuna contra el cáncer del pulmón," *20 minutos*, January 11, 2011.

78. Agence France Presse, "Cuba presenta nueva vacuna contra el cáncer," January 2, 2013.

79. Agencia Cubana de Noticias, "Un expert des États-Unis se déclare intéressé par une collaboration avec Cuba," December 13, 2011.

80. Campion and Morrissey, "A Different Model: Medical Care in Cuba."

81. "Directora general de la UNESCO constata logros de la biotecnología cubana," *Juventud Rebelde*, November 29, 2012.

82. Ladys Marlene León Corrales, "Valor social de la Misión Milagro en el contexto venezolano," *Biblioteca Virtual en Salud de Cuba*, March 2009, http://bvs.sld.cu/revistas/spu/vol35_4_09/spu06409.htm.

83. Felipe Pérez Roque, "Discurso del canciller de Cuba en la ONU," *Bohemia Digital*, November 9, 2006.

84. CSC News, "Medical Brigades Have Treated 85 Million," April 4, 2008, http://www.cuba-solidarity.org.uk/news.asp?ItemID=1288.

85. "L'ONU déclare la transmission du sida de la mère à l'enfant officiellement éradiquée à Cuba," *Granma*, June 21, 2012.

86. José A. de la Osa, "Egresa 11 mil médicos de Universidades cubanas," *Granma*, July 11, 2012.

87. Elizabeth Newhouse, "Disaster Medicine: U.S. Doctors Examine Cuba's Approach," Center for International Policy, July 9, 2012, http://www.ciponline.org/research/html/disaster-medicine-us-doctors-examine-cubas-approach.

88. de la Osa, "Egresa 11 mil médicos de Universidades cubanas"; Ministerio de Relaciones Exteriores, "Graduados por la Revolución más de 100 000 médicos," July 16, 2009.

89. Organisation mondiale de la santé (WHO), "Cuba: Health Profile," 2010, http://www.who.int/gho/countries/cub.pdf; Newhouse, "Disaster Medicine: U.S. Doctors Examine Cuba's Approach."

90. de la Osa, "Egresa 11 mil médicos de Universidades cubanas."

91. Organisation mondiale de la santé, "Cuba répond à la demande de médecins," May 1, 2010, http://www.who.int/bulletin/volumes/88/5/10-010510/fr/index.html.

92. Escuela Latinoamericana de Medicina de Cuba, "Historia de la ELAM."

93. Agencia cubana de noticias, "Over 15,000 Foreign Physicians Graduated in Cuba in Seven Years," July 14, 2012.
94. Organisation mondiale de la santé, "Cuba répond à la demande de médecins."
95. Programme des Nations Unies pour le Développement, *Investigación sobre ciencia, tecnología y desarrollo humano en Cuba*, 2003, 117–19, http://www.undp.org.cu/idh percent20cuba/cap6.pdf.
96. Ibid.
97. Programa de Naciones Unidas para el Desarrollo, "Objetivos de desarrollo del Milenio en Venezuela," 2011, http://www.pnud.org. ve/content/view/176/169/ (site consulted January 7, 2012).
98. Programme des Nations Unies pour le Développement, *Investigación sobre ciencia, tecnología y desarrollo humano en Cuba*.
99. Programme des Nations unies pour le Développement, *Rapport sur le développement humain 2011* (New York: Nations Unies, 2011), 150, http://hdr.undp.org/en/media/HDR_2011_FR_Complete.pdf.
100. Programa de Naciones Unidas para el Desarrollo, "Objetivos de desarrollo del Milenio en Venezuela," 2011.
101. Fidel Ernesto Vásquez, "Petrocaribe promueve el intercambio justo y equitativo en la región," Partido Socialista Unido de Venezuela, October 27, 2011, http://aristobulo.psuv.org.ve/2011/10/27/ canpana/petrocaribe-promueve-el-intercambio-justo-y-equita-tivo-en-la-region/.
102. Ministerio de Relaciones Exteriores, "Alcanza la 'Operación Milagro' en Bolivia más de 600 000 operaciones de la vista," *República de Cuba*, August 29, 2011.
103. Programme des Nations Unies pour le Développement, "Taux de mortalité infantile chez les moins de cinq ans (pour 1000 naissances vivantes)," (Paris: Nations Unies, 2011).
104. Presidencia de la República, "100 logros del Gobierno para Bolivia (2006-2009)," *Estado Plurinacional de Bolivia*, 2010, http://www. presidencia.gob.bo/documentos/logros100.pdf.
105. Programme des Nations Unies pour le Développement, *Rapport sur le développement humain 2011*, 150.
106. Mariela Pérez Valenzuela, "ALBA: la justicia de los hechos," *Granma*, July 14, 2009, http://www.granma.cubaweb.cu/secciones/ alba/int/2integ32.html.
107. Programme des Nations Unies pour le Développement, *Rapport sur le développement humain 2011*, 150.
108. Pedro Rioseco, "Ecuador. Destacan logros de Revolución Ciudadana

en cuatro años," *Prensa Latina*, May 31, 2011.

109. Programme des Nations Unies pour le Développement, *Rapport sur le développement humain 2011*, 150.

110. Presidencia de la República de Ecuador, "En 4 años, Gobierno aspira a declarar Ecuador país libre de desnutrición infantil," *El Ciudadano*, October 27, 2011; UNICEF, *Progreso para la infancia: Un balance sobre la nutrición*, 2011.

111. Henry Reeve, a U.S. citizen who rose to become a brigadier general in the Ejercito Libertador during the first Cuban War of Independence between 1868 and 1878, gave his life for the liberation of the island.

112. Felipe Pérez Roque, "Discurso del canciller de Cuba en la ONU," *Bohemia Digital*, November 9, 2006.

113. Ibid.

114. Nina Lakhani, "Cuban Medics in Haiti Put the World to Shame," *The Independent*, December 26, 2010.

115. *CubaDebate*, "Presentan filme sobre cooperación cubana en el Pacífico," November 10, 2009.

116. Tom Fawthrop, "Impoverished Cuba Sends Doctors Around the Globe to Help the Poor," *Syndney Morning Herald*, October 28, 2006.

117. Ibid.

118. Institut national de sciences de l'univers, "Séïsme de Haïti du 12 janvier 2010," Centre national de la recherche scientifique, January 19, 2010, http://www.insu.cnrs.fr/co/terre-solide/catastrophes-et-risques/seismes/seisme-de-haiti-du-12-janvier-2010.

119. Radio Canada, "Le bilan grimpe à 230 000 morts," February 10, 2010, http://www.radio-canada.ca/nouvelles/International/2010/02/10/004-haiti_bilan.shtml.

120. Lakhani, "Cuban Medics in Haiti Put the World to Shame."

121. Andrés Martínez Casares, "Cuba Takes Lead Role in Haiti's Cholera Fight," *New York Times*, November 7, 2011.

122. Ibid. Also see *CubaDebate*, "Brigada Médica Cubana en Haití alcanza records mínimos de tasa de letalidad por cólera," March 5, 2011.

123. "Terremoto en Haití," *El País*, 2010, http://www.elpais.com/especial/terremoto-haiti-2010/.

124. "Ayuda financiera y equipos de asistencia," *El País*, April 15, 2010.

125. Escuela Latinoamericana de Medicina de Cuba, "Historia de la ELAM."

126. Programme des Nations Unies pour le Développement, *Investigación sobre ciencia, tecnología y desarrollo humano en Cuba*, 2003, 117–19, http://www.undp.org.cu/idh percent20cuba/cap6.pdf.
127. Organisation mondiale de la santé, "Cécité et déficience visuelle," Summary no. 282, October 2011, http://www.who.int/mediacentre/factsheets/fs282/fr/index.html.
128. Ministerio de Relaciones Exteriores, "Celebra Operación Milagro cubana en Guatemala," *República de Cuba*, November 15, 2010; Operación Milagro, "¿Qué es la Operación Milagro?" http://www.operacionmilagro.org.ar/.
129. Ministerio de Relaciones Exteriores, "Celebra Cuba el millón de pacientes de Operación Milagro," *República de Cuba*, January 24, 2008. For U.S. citizens who benefited from this humanitarian program, see "Oftalmólogo estadounidense reconoce valor de Operación Milagro," *Prensa Latina*, January 19, 2007.
130. Operación Milagro, "¿Qué es la Operación Milagro?"
131. Ministerio de Relaciones Exteriores, "Alcanza la 'Operación Milagro' en Bolivia más de 600 000 operaciones de la vista," *República de Cuba*, August 29, 2011; Agence France Presse, "Médicos cubanos operaron de la vista a más de 600,000 bolivianos," February 11, 2013.
132. Ministerio de Relaciones Exteriores, "Destaca Evo Morales ejemplo solidario de Misión Milagro," *República de Cuba*, September 1, 2011.
133. Ministerio de Relaciones Exteriores, "Cien mil ecuatorianos beneficiados por la Operación Milagro," February 2, 2010. http://www.cubaminrex.cu/Cooperacion/2010/0202_2.html (site consulted November 13, 2011).
134. *CubaDebate,* "Más de 61 mil nicaragüenses atendidos por médicos cubanos," February 8, 2010.
135. *CubaDebate,* "Más de 61 mil jamaicanos atendidos por oftalmólogos cubanos," May 26, 2011.
136. Ministerio de Relaciones Exteriores, "Reconocen importancia de Operación Milagro para población panameña," *República de Cuba*, February 1, 2010.
137. *CubaDebate*, "Médicos cubanos realizaron 600 mil cirugías de ojos en Bolivia," September 5, 2011.
138. "Oftalmólogo estadounidense reconoce valor de Operación Milagro," *Prensa Latina*, January 19, 2007.
139. Héctor Arturo, "Che vuelve a ganar otro combate," *Granma*, September 29, 2007.

142   Notes to pages 48-52

140. Juan Pablo Meneses, "¡Primicia Mundial! Entrevista a Pablo Ortiz," *Crónicas Argentinas*, October 11, 2006.
141. *CubaDebate*, "Operación Milagro, Premio a la Excelencia Ciudadana en Uruguay," August 21, 2009.
142. *Info 690*, "Des Québécois qui se font soigner à Cuba," April 7, 2008; Radio Canada, "Tourisme médical à Cuba," January 9, 2012, http:// www.youtube.com/watch?v=YAJSqmE6DWI.
143. Halla Thorsteinsdóttir and Tirso W. Sáenz, "Tackling Meningitis in Africa," *Science*, December 2, 2012, 1546-47; Jorge Manzaneda, "Vacunas de Cuba y Brasil salvan miles de vidas en Africa," *Trabajadores*, January, 10, 2013.
144. Ibid.
145. Ibid.
146. Thorsteinsdóttir and Sáenz, "Tackling Meningitis in Africa."
147. Jaime Pratts, "La vacuna contra la tuberculosis se probará en humanos este año," *El País*, February 29, 2012.
148. UNESCO, *La crise cachée: Les conflits armés et l'éducation*, Rapport mondial 2011 (Paris: Nations Unies, 2011), 72, http://unesdoc. unesco.org/images/0019/001917/191794f.pdf.
149. Ibid., 37, 76.
150. Ibid., 39.
151. Leonela Inés Relys Díaz, "La alfabetización por radio y televisión," *Yo sí puedo*, http://yosipuedo.com.ar/art-leonela.htm.
152. Correspondance with Professeur Carlos M. Molina Soto, November 17, 2011.
153. Antonio Rodrigo Torrijos, "Torrijos pregunta en el pleno del Ayuntamiento sobre el futuro de Yo, sí puedo: Al pleno del Ayuntamiento de Sevilla," September 15, 2011. See also "Alfabetización cubana en Sevilla," *Cubainformación*, February 7, 2008, http://www.cubainformacion.tv/index.php?option=com_con tent&task=view&id=3286&Itemid=86.
154. EFE, "Un método desarrollado en Cuba enseña a leer y a escribir a aborígenes australianos," July 1, 2012.
155. Programme des Nations Unies pour le développement, "Indice de développement humain IDH, classement 2011," 2011, http://hdr. undp.org/fr/statistiques/.
156. "Reconoce la UNESCO el método cubano de alfabetización," *Granma*, May 25, 2011.
157. *Rebelión*, "IU reclama el mantenimiento del programa de alfa- betización 'Yo, sí puedo' en Sevilla," September 11, 2011, http://

rebelion.org/noticia.php?id=135382; Antonio Ernesto Guzman, "Plus de 7 millions de personnes ont appris à lire et à écrire grâce à 'Yo, sí puedo,'" *Granma*, April 24, 2013.

158. "Reconoce la UNESCO el método cubano de alfabetización," *Granma*, May 25, 2011.

159. Ministerio de Relaciones Exteriores de la República de Cuba, "Más de 18 mil niños de Chernobyl atendidos en Cuba," March 2005.

160. Reuters, "Chernobyl Victims Treated in Cuba," March 23, 2010.

161. Andrés Schipani, "Revolutionary Care: Castro's Doctors Give Hope to the Children of Chernobyl," *The Guardian*, July 2, 2009.

162. Fernando Ravsberg, "Cuba: 15 años con víctimas de Chernobyl," BBC, http://news.bbc.co.uk/hi/spanish/latin_america/newsid_441 6000/4416823.stm.

163. Ministerio de Relaciones Exteriores de la República de Cuba, "Más de 18 mil niños de Chernobyl atendidos en Cuba."

164. "Atendidos 18,000 niños de Chernobyl," *El Nuevo Herald*, March 31, 2005.

165. Ministerio de Relaciones Exteriores de la República de Cuba, "Más de 18 mil niños de Chernobyl atendidos en Cuba."

166. "Ukraine Thanks Cuba for Helping Chernobyl Victims," *China Daily*, December 24, 2010, http://www.chinadaily.com.cn/world/2010-12/24/content_11751208.htm (site consulted January 3, 2013).

167. Radio Habana Cuba, "Un haut fonctionnaire de l'ONU signale que Cuba est le pays le plus sûr de l'Amérique latine," May 25, 2012.

168. Fernando Ravsberg, "Cómo consigue Cuba hacer frente a la devastación de los huracanes," *Público*, October 31, 2012, http://www.publico.es/internacional/444694/como-consigue-cuba-hacer-frente-a-la-devastacion-de-los-huracanes.

169. Ibid.

170. Ibid.

171. Newhouse, "Disaster Medicine: U.S. Doctors Examine Cuba's Approach."

172. Ibid.

173. Rui Dong, "FAO reconoce trabajo de Cuba por desarrollo agrícola," *Xinhua*, May 20, 2012, http://spanish.china.org.cn/international/txt/2012-05/20/content_25424980.htm.

174. FAO, *L'état de l'insécurité alimentaire dans le monde 2012*, 2012, http://www.fao.org/publications/sofi/fr/.

175. *Mesa Redonda*, "Alaba experto de la FAO logros alimentarios de Cuba," November 23, 2012, http://mesaredonda.

cubadebate.cu/noticias/2012/11/23/alaba-experto-de-la-fao-logros-alimentarios-de-cuba/.

176. José Graziano Da Silva, "Carta a Fidel Castro," Organisation des Nations Unies pour l'alimentation et l'agriculture, April 29, 2013, http://www.cubadebate.cu/noticias/2013/05/06/carta-a-fidel-del-director-general-de-la-fao/.

177. "La superficie des forêts augmente dans l'île," *Granma*, December 27, 2006.

178. *Energy Globe*, "National Energy Globe Winners," 2006; Agencia Cubana de Noticias, "Le projet cubain d'énergie renouvelable gagne le Prix mondial 'Energy Globe,'" January 29, 2007.

179. World Wildlife Fund, *Planète vivante 2006*, Rapport, 2006, 21.

180. Piero Gleijeses, *Misiones en conflicto. La Habana, Washington y África 1959–1976* (Havana: Editorial de Ciencias Sociales, 2004), 55.

181. Nelson Mandela, "Discours de Nelson Mandela à La Havane," Matanzas, Cuba, July 26, 1991, http://romancatholicworld.files.wordpress.com/2013/12/castro-speech-data-base-latin-american-network-information-center-lanic.pdf

182. Dan Erikson, Annie Lord, and Peter Wolf, *Cuba's Social Services: A Review of Education, Health, and Sanitation* (Washington, DC: World Bank, 2002), 3.

183. Raquel Marrero Yanes, "Cuba muestra indicadores sociales y demográficos de países desarrollados," *Granma*, July 12, 2012.

184. Mauricio Vicent, "Cuba se resiste a normalizar las relaciones con la UE," *El País*, October 28, 2010.

185. Salim Lamrani, *Double Morale: Cuba, l'Union européenne et les droits de l'homme* (Paris: Editions Estrella, 2008).

186. Amnesty International, *Rapport 2011: La situation des droits humains dans le monde*, 2011, http://files.amnesty.org/air11/air_2011_full_fr.pdf.

187. Amnesty International, "Amnesty International Reaction to Release of Activists in Cuba," March 23, 2011, http://www.amnesty.org/en/for-media/press-releases/amnesty-international-reaction-release-activists-cuba-2011-03-23; Amnesty International, *Rapport 2012: La situation des droits humains dans le monde*, 2012, http://www.amnesty.org/fr/annual-report/2012.

188. Amnesty International, *Rapport 2011*.

189. Mauricio Vicent, "Cuba libera tres presos al vencer el plazo para las excarcelaciones," *El País*, November 7, 2010.

190. Mauricio Vicent, "Cuba libera a Biscet, el preso más emblemático del Grupo de los 75," *El País*, March 11, 2003.

191. Amnesty International, *Rapport 2011*.

192. Cuban Democracy Act, Title17, Article 1705, 1992.

193. Helms-Burton Act, Title 1, Article 109, 1996.

194. Colin L. Powell, *Commission for Assistance to a Free Cuba* (Washington, DC: U.S. Department of State, May 2004), 16, 22.

195. Roger F. Noriega, "Assistant Secretary Noriega's Statement Before the House of Representatives Committee on International Relations," U.S. Department of State, March 3, 2005.

196. Condoleezza Rice and Carlos Gutierrez, *Commission for Assistance to a Free Cuba* (Washington, DC: U.S. Department of State, July 2006).

197. Ibid., 22.

198. *Along the Malecon*, "Exclusive: Q & A with USAID," October 25, 2010, http://alongthemalecon.blogspot.com/2010/10/exclusive-q-with-usaid.html.

199. Ibid.

200. Ibid.

201. "Cuba: EEUU debe tomar medidas contra diplomáticos," Associated Press/*El Nuevo Herald*, May 19, 2008.

202. Michael Parmly, "How to Shatter a Castro-Phile's Arguments," U.S. Interests Section, June 28, 2007, cable 07HAVANA617, http://wikileaks.org/cable/2007/06/07HAVANA617.html.

203. "Disidente cubana teme que pueda ser encarcelada," *El Nuevo Herald*, May 21, 2008.

204. Patrick Bèle, "Cuba accuse Washington de payer les dissidents," *Le Figaro*, May 21, 2008.

205. Agence France-Presse, "Prensa estatal cubana hace inusual entrevista callejera a disidentes," May 22, 2008.

206. Tracey Eaton, "Factions Spar Over U.S. Aid for Cuba," *Houston Chronicle*, December 18, 2010.

207. Agence France-Presse, "Financement de la dissidence: Cuba somme Washington de s'expliquer," May 22, 2008.

208. EFE, "Un diputado cubano propone nuevos castigos a opositores pagados por EE UU," May 28, 2008.

209. Jeff Franks, "Top U.S. Diplomat Ferried Cash to Dissident: Cuba," Reuters, May 19, 2008.

210. Ben Feller, "Bush Touts Cuban Life After Castro," Associated Press, October 24, 2007.

211. Will Weissert, "Activistas cubanos dependen del financiamiento extranjero," Associated Press, August 15, 2008.
212. Félix Rousseau, "Fariñas, épine dans le pied de Raúl Castro," *Libération*, March 17, 2010.
213. Jonathan D. Farrar, "Request for HRDF Funds for Cuban Organizations," U.S. Interests Section, Havana, July 31, 2008, cable 08HAVANA613, http://www.cablegatesearch.net/cable.php?id=08HAVANA613&version=1315488573.
214. Amnesty International, "Cuba: Cinq années de trop, le nouveau gouvernement doit libérer les dissidents emprisonnés," March 18, 2008, http://www.amnesty.org/fr/for-media/press-releases/cuba-five-years-too-many-new-government-must-release-jailed-dissidents-2.
215. Joaquin F. Monserrate, "Feisty Little Missions Dent Cuba's Record of Bullying Others to Silence on Human Rights," U.S. Interests Section, November 9, 2009, cable 09HAVANA706, http://213.251.145.96/cable/2009/11/09HAVANA706.html (site consulted December 18, 2010).
216. Joaquin F. Monserrate, "GOC Signals 'Readiness to Move Forward'," U.S. Interests Section, September 25, 2009, cable 09HAVANA592, http://213.251.145.96/cable/2009/09/09HAVANA592.html.
217. Jonathan D. Farrar, "The U.S. and the Role of the Opposition in Cuba," U.S. Interests Section, April 9, 2009, cable 09HAVANA221, http://213.251.145.96/cable/2009/04/09HAVANA221.html.
218. Michael E. Parmly, "Comsec Discusses Freedom and Democracy With Cuban Youth," U.S. Interests Section, January 18, 2008, 08HAVANA66, http://213.251.145.96/cable/2008/01/08HAVANA66.html.
219. Jonathan D. Farrar, "The Speculation on Fidel's Health," U.S. Interests Section, January 9, 2009, cable 09HAVANA35, http://213.251.145.96/cable/2009/01/09HAVANA35.html.
220. Farrar, "The U.S. and the Role of the Opposition in Cuba."
221. Ibid.
222. Ibid.
223. Ibid.
224. Joaquin F. Monserrate, "GOC Signals 'Readiness to Move Forward'," U.S. Interests Section, September 25, 2009, cable 09HAVANA592, http://213.251.145.96/cable/2009/09/09HAVANA592.html.
225. Jonathan D. Farrar, "Key Trading Parters See No Big Economic Reforms," U.S. Interests Section, February 9, 2010, cable 10HAVANA84, http://213.251.145.96/cable/2010/02/10HAVANA84.html.

226. Farrar, "The U.S. and the Role of the Opposition in Cuba."

227. Ibid.

228. Ibid.

229. Farrar, "Key Trading Parters See No Big Economic Reforms."

230. Jonathan D. Farrar, "How Might Cuba Enter Another Special Period?" U.S. Interests Section, June 4, 2009, http://213.251.145.96/cable/2009/06/09HAVANA322.html.

231. Parmly, "Comsec Discusses Freedom and Democracy With Cuban Youth."

232. Radio Habana Cuba, "Former Chief of US Interests Section in Havana Wayne Smith Says Sending Money to Mercenaries in Cuba is Illegal," May 21, 2008.

233. Wayne S. Smith, "New Cuba Commission Report: Formula for Continued Failure," Center for International Policy, July 10, 2006.

234. BBC, "Cuba Ladies In White Protest Blocked in Havana," September 24, 2011.

235. Paul Haven, "Number of Political Prisoners in Cuba Still Murky," Associated Press, July 23, 2010.

236. Juan O. Tamayo, "¿Cuántos presos políticos hay en la isla?" *El Nuevo Herald*, July 22, 2010.

237. José Luis Fraga, "Alarcón: Presos liberados pueden quedarse en Cuba y podrían ser más de 52," Agence France-Presse, July 20, 2010.

238. Haven, "Number of Political Prisoners in Cuba Still Murky."

239. EFE, "España pide a UE renovar relación con Cuba," July 27, 2010.

240. Juan Carlos Chávez, "Opositores discrepan del cardenal Ortega," *El Nuevo Herald*, October 29, 2011.

241. EFE, "Cuba Still Holding Political Prisoners, Dissidents Say," November 23, 2011.

242. "*El País* convoca los Premios Ortega y Gasset de periodismo 2009," *El País*, January 12, 2009.

243. Yoani Sánchez, "Negocio de familia," *El País*, September 7, 2011; Yoani Sánchez, "Querido Pablo," *El País*, August 27, 2011; Yoani Sánchez, "Ignacio y Wendy se casan," *El País*, August 20, 2011, etc.

244. Ibid.

245. Yoani Sánchez, "Mi perfil," *Generación Y*.

246. Ibid.

247. Yoani Sánchez, "La improbable entrevista de Gianni Miná," *Generación Y*, May 9, 2009.

248. Yoani Sánchez, "Vine y me quedé," *Generación Y*, August 14, 2007.

249. Ibid.

250. Correspondance with his Excellency Orlando Requeijo, Ambassador of the Republic of Cuba, to Paris, November 18, 2009.

251. *Libertad Digital*, "Yoani Sánchez: 'Hemos naufragado; hace rado que estamos bajo el agua,'" November 12, 2009, http://www.libertaddigital.com/mundo/yoani-sanchez-desde-que-comence-a-escribir-el-blog-vivo-un-thriller-de-accion-1276375966/.

252. "Ce pays est une immense prison avec des murs idéologiques," *France 24.com*, October 22, 2009.

253. "Cuba: las últimas imágenes del naufragio," *El Nuevo Día*, September 18, 2011, http://www.elnuevodia.com/cubalasultimasimagenesdel-naufragio..-1069420.html.

254. Yoani Sánchez, "Siete preguntas," *Generación Y*, November 18, 2009.

255. Yoani Sánchez, "Seres de la sombra," *Generación Y*, November 12, 2009.

256. *El Nuevo Día*, "Cuba: las últimas imágenes del naufragio."

257. *Libertad Digital*, "Yoani Sánchez: 'Hemos naufragado; hace rado que estamos bajo el agua.'"

258. Mauricio Vicent, "Los cambios llegarán a Cuba, pero no a través del guión del Gobierno," *El País*, May 7, 2008.

259. Salim Lamrani, "Conversations avec la bloggeuse cubaine Yoani Sánchez," April 15, 2010, *Voltairenet*, http://www.voltairenet.org/article164956.html#article164956. Yoani Sánchez on economic sanctions.

260. Ibid.

261. Yoani Sánchez, "Made in USA," *Generación Y*, November 18, 2009.

262. Lamrani, "Conversations avec la bloggeuse cubaine Yoani Sánchez." Yoaní Sánchez on the shared goal with the United States.

263. *El Nuevo Día*, "Cuba: las últimas imágenes del naufragio."

264. Lamrani, "Conversations avec la bloggeuse cubaine Yoani Sánchez."

265. Yoani Sánchez, "Premios," *Generación Y*.

266. Yoani Sánchez, "¿Qué hago yo ahí," *Generación Y*, May 3, 2008.

267. Norelys Morales Aguilera, "Si los blogs son terapéuticos ¿Quién paga la terapia de Yoani Sánchez?" *La República*, August 13, 2009.

268. Yoani Sánchez, *Generación Y*.

269. Aguilera, "Si los blogs son terapéuticos ¿Quién paga la terapia de Yoani Sánchez?"

270. Joaquin F. Monserrate, "GOC Signals 'Readiness to Move Forward,'" U.S. Interests Section, September 25, 2009, cable 09HAVANA592, http://213.251.145.96/cable/2009/09/09HAVANA592.html.

271. Michael Parmly, "Consenso OnLine: An Impartial Forum in Cuba?" U.S. Interests Section, June 28, 2007, cable 07HAVANA622, http://wikileaks.org/cable/2007/06/07HAVANA622.html.

272. Stéphane Bussard, "Ma rencontre avec l'auteur des câbles sur Cuba," *Le Temps*, December 30, 2010.

273. Jonathan D. Farrar, "Questions From Yoani Sánchez to POTUS," August 28, 2009, cable 09HAVANA527, http://wikileaks.org/cable/2009/08/09HAVANA527.html.

274. Yoani Sánchez, https://twitter.com/yoanisanchez.

275. Ibid.

276. *Followerwonk*, "Twitter Analytics: Find, Analyze, and Optimize for Social Growth," http://followerwonk.com/.

277. Claudia Herrera Beltrán, "El ciberacarreo, la nueva estrategia de los políticos en Twitter," *La Jornada*, January 30, 2012.

278. Joseba Elola, "Perfiles con muchos 'huevos'," *El País*, April 22, 2012.

279. Yoani Sánchez, "A la distancia de un CLIC," *Generación Y*, June 28, 2012, http://www.desdecuba.com/generaciony/.

280. Yoani Sánchez, "El futuro con Mariela Castro," *Generación Y*, May 28, 2012, http://www.desdecuba.com/generaciony/.

281. Yoani Sánchez, "Fuenteovejuna," *Generación Y*, June 13, 2012, http://www.desdecuba.com/generaciony/.

282. Yoani Sánchez, "¿Buen talante?" *Generación Y*, June 12, 2012, http://www.desdecuba.com/generaciony/.

283. Yoani Sánchez, "Cerdo en 'cajita'," *Generación Y*, May 16, 2012, http://www.desdecuba.com/generaciony/.

284. Yoani Sánchez, "Los nuevos chefs de La Habana: Los 10 mejores restaurantes de la renovada cocina cubana," *El País*, July 23, 2012, http://elviajero.elpais.com/elviajero/2012/07/23/actualidad/134305 7020_608376.html.

285. "Nombran a Yoani en Comisión de la SIP," *El Nuevo Herald*, November 9, 2012.

286. Taxi from La Habana Vieja to Playa.

287. Eighty-five percent of all Cubans own their homes. This rate is reserved exclusively for citizens of the island.

288. 0.09 CUP/kilowatt/hour to 100 kilowatt/hour.

289. 0.35 CUP/m^3.

290. 0.11 CUP/m^3.

291. Jonathan D. Farrar, "Blogger Thrilled With POTUS Response to Her Q&As," November 9, 2009, cable 09HAVANA695, http://wikileaks.org/cable/2009/11/09HAVANA695.html.

292. Mauricio Vicent, "Artistas de EE UU piden a Washington que excarcele a cinco agentes cubanos," *El País*, September 23, 2010.

293. David Alandete, "Fidel Castro arremete contra el gesto de apertura de Obama," *El País*, September 30, 2011.

294. Yolanda Monge, "Liberado un cubano acusado de espionaje en Estados Unidos," *El País*, October 7, 2011.

295. Fabián Escalante Font, *The Secret War: CIA Covert Operations Against Cuba 1959-1962* (Melbourne: Ocean Press, 1995).

296. Gobierno de Cuba, "Demanda del pueblo de Cuba al gobierno de Estados Unidos por daños humanos," *República de Cuba*, May 31, 1999, http://www.cubagob.cu/ingles/rel_ext/demanda.htm.

297. Federal Bureau of Investigation, "Bombing of Cubana Airlines DC-8 Near Barbados, West Indies, October 6, 1976, Neutrality Matters, Cuba-West Indies," November 1976, Luis Posada Carriles, Declassified Record, National Security Archive, George Washington University, http://www.gwu.edu/~nsarchiv/NSAEBB/NSAEBB153/19761102.pdf; Federal Bureau of Investigation, "Suspected Bombing of Cubana Airlines DC-8 Near Barbados, West Indies, October 6, 1976," October 7, 1976, Luis Posada Carriles, Declassified Record, National Security Archive, George Washington University, http://www.gwu.edu/~nsarchiv/NSAEBB/NSAEBB153/19761008.pdf.

298. James LeMoyne, "Cuban Linked to Terror Bombings Is Freed by Government in Miami," Editorial, July 18, 1990; *New York Times* "The Bosch Case Does Violence to Justice," *New York Times*, July 20, 1990.

299. Salim Lamrani, *Fidel Castro, Cuba et les Etats-Unis* (Pantin: Le Temps des Cerises, 2006).

300. Ann Louise Bardach and Larry Rohter, "Key Cuba Foe Claims Exiles' Backing," *New York Times*, July 12, 1998.

301. Central Intelligence Agency, "Personal Record Questionnaire on Posada," January 21, 1972, Luis Posada Carriles, Declassified Record, National Security Archive, George Washington University, http://www.gwu.edu/~nsarchiv/NSAEBB/NSAEBB153/19720417.pdf; Central Intelligence Agency, "Suspected Bombing of Cubana Airlines DC-8 Near Barbados, West Indies, October 6, 1976," Luis Posada Carriles, Declassified Record, National Security Archive, George Washington University, http://www.gwu.edu/~nsarchiv/NSAEBB/NSAEBB153/19761016.pdf; Central Intelligence Agency, "Luis Pozada," June 7, 1966, Luis Posada Carriles, Declassified

Record, National Security Archive, George Washington University, http://www.gwu.edu/~nsarchiv/NSAEBB/NSAEBB153/19660600. pdf.

302. Raúl Castro Ruz, "Discurso pronunciado por el General de Ejército Raúl Castro Ruz, Presidente de los Consejos de Estado y de Ministros, en el acto por el Día de las víctimas del Terrorismo de Estado, efectuado en la Sala Universal de las FAR," October 6, 2010, http://www.cubadebate.cu/Raúl-castro-ruz/2010/10/06/el-gobierno-cubano-insta-al-presidente-obama-a-que-sea-consecuente-con-su-compromiso-en-la-lucha-antiterrorista/.

303. *Antiterroristas*, "Who Are They?" http://www.antiterroristas.cu/en/who-are-they.

304. Tracey Eaton, "FBI Examined U.S.-Made Detonators in Cuba after 1997 Bombings," *Along the Malecon*, May 20, 2010, http://alongthemalecon.blogspot.com/2010/05/fbi-examined-us-made-detonators-in-cuba.html.

305. *Antiterroristas*, "The Trial," http://www.antiterroristas.cu/en/trial.

306. Ibid.

307. Ibid.

308. Ibid.

309. Ibid.

310. Ibid.

311. Ibid.

312. *La Jiribilla*, "El padre de la criatura y los techos de vidrio," http://www.lajiribilla.cu/2005/n194_01/194_13.html.

313. "Details revealed of U.S. government efforts to deny the Cuban Five a fair trial," *Granma*, August 24, 2012.

314. "Miedo a ser jurado en juicio de espías," *El Nuevo Herald*, December 2, 2000.

315. Salim Lamrani, *Fidel Castro, Cuba et les Etats-Unis* (Pantin: Le Temps des Cerises, 2006).

316. *Antiterroristas*, "Statements by Witnesses and Experts During the 2001 Trial," http://www.antiterroristas.cu/index.php?option=com_content&view=article&id=543&Itemid=106.

317. Lamrani, *Fidel Castro, Cuba et les États-Unis*, 83–85.

318. Ibid., 85.

319. Rafael Hojas Martínez, "Un abracadabra de millones: Entrevista a Ricardo Alarcón de Quesada, Presidente de la Asamblea Nacional del Poder Popular," *Trabajadores*, September 11, 2011; Ricardo Alarcón de Quesada, "Un 'asesinato'

fabricado: Una extraña investigación," *CubaDebate*, September 12, 2012, http://www.cubadebate.cu/opinion/2012/09/12/un-asesinato-fabricado-una-extrana-investigacion/.

320. Monge, "Liberado un cubano acusado de espionaje en Estados Unidos."
321. Oscar Haza, "A mano limpia," *Canal 41*, December 6, 2005.
322. Lamrani, *Fidel Castro, Cuba et les Etats-Unis*.
323. *Antiterroristas*, "The Trial "
324. Federal Bureau of Investigation, "Robert Philip Hanssen Espionage Case," February 20, 2001, http://www.fbi.gov/about-us/history/famous-cases/robert-hanssen.
325. *Antiterroristas*, "The Trial."
326. *Antiterroristas*, "The Appeal ," http://www.antiterroristas.cu/en/appeal.
327. Ibid.
328. Ibid.
329. *Antiterroristas*, "The Supreme Court," http://www.antiterroristas.cu/en/supreme-court.
330. *Antiterroristas*, "The Resentencing Process," http://www.antiterroristas.cu/en/resentencing-process.
331. *Antiterroristas*, "The Collateral Appeal (Habeas Corpus)," http://www.antiterroristas.cu/en/collateral-appeal-habeas-corpus.
332. Salim Lamrani, "50 verdades sobre el caso de los 5," *Opera Mundi*, October 30, 2013, http://operamundi.uol.com.br/conteudo/babel/32141/50+verdades+sobre+el+caso+de+los+5.shtml.
333. *Antiterroristas*, "René González's Supervised Release," http://www.antiterroristas.cu/en/rene-gonzalezs-supervised-release.
334. Wayne S. Smith, "The Case of the Cuban Five: The U.S. Shame and How to End It," Center for International Policy, June 15, 2010, http://www.ciponline.org/research/entry/cuban-five-us-shame.
335. Lawrence Wilkerson, "The Cuban Five," *The Havana Note*, September 19, 2007, http://thehavananote.com/2007/09/cuban_five (website consulted December 30, 2013).
336. *Antiterroristas*, "Human Rights Organizations," http://www.antiterroristas.cu/en/human-rights-organizations.
337. Wilfredo Cancio Isla, "Posada Carriles podría quedar en libertad condicional," *El Nuevo Herald*, April 17, 2007; Associated Press, "Cuban Militant Posada Posts $250K Bail," April 18, 2007; Ian James, "Lawyer: U.S. Protecting Cuban Militant," Associated Press, April 9, 2007; Associated Press, "Judge Rejects Bid to Delay Bond

Order For Anti-Castro Militant," April 10, 2007; Fabiola Sanchez, "Venezuelan Military Agents Raid Home of Friend of Anti-Castro Militant Posada," Associated Press, April 13, 2007; Tim Weiner, "Cuban Exile Is Charged With Illegal Entry," *New York Times*, May 20, 2005; Reuters, "Castro Accuses Bush of Protecting Accused Bomber," April 10, 2007; Spencer S. Hsu and Nick Miroff, "U.S. Holds Suspects in War Crimes," *Washington Post*, April 4, 2007; Jeff Franks, "Anti-Castro Exile Freed En Route to Miami," Reuters, April 19, 2007; *Los Angeles Times*, "U.S. Loses Bid to Keep Posada Jailed," April 18, 2007; *USA Today*, "Cuba, Venezuela Protest Pending Release of Anti-Communist," April 11, 2007; *Boston Globe*, "Caracas Demands US Return of Militant," May 21, 2005; Eric Leser, "L'arrestation de l'anticastriste Luis Posada Carriles, à Miami, embarrasse les Etats-Unis," *Le Monde*, April 6, 2007; Jean-Hébert Armengaud, "Cuba réclame une figure anticastriste arrêtée aux Etats-Unis," *Libération*, May 19, 2005.

338. Mauricio Vicent, "Cuba condena a un contratista de EE UU a 15 años de cárcel," *El País*, March 13, 2011.

339. Andrea Rodriguez, "Judíos niegan haber colaborado con Alan Gross," Associated Press, December 2, 2010.

340. Jewish Telegraphic Agency, "Cuba to Seek 20-Year Prison Term for Alan Gross," February 6, 2011.

341. Andrea Rodriguez, "EEUU pide iglesias de Cuba interesarse por contratista preso," Associated Press, December 2, 2010.

342. Jewish Telegraphic Agency, "Clinton Makes Plea for Cuban Detainee Alan Gross," July 14, 2010.

343. Arturo López-Levy, "Freeing Alan Gross: First Do No Harm," *The Washington Note,* August 26, 2010.

344. Wayne S. Smith, "The Gross Case and the Inanity of U.S. Policy," Center for International Policy, March 2011.

345. Desmond Butler, "AP Impact: USAID Contractor Work in Cuba Detailed," *The Guardian*, February 12, 2012, http://www.guardian.co.uk/world/feedarticle/10089898.

346. Ibid.

347. "Aumenta el número de cubanos que intenta llegar a Estados Unidos," *El País*, October 9, 2011.

348. Office of Immigration Statistics, U.S. Department of Homeland Security, "2010 Yearbook of Immigration Statistics," August 2011, 5–15. http://www.dhs.gov/xlibrary/assets/statistics/yearbook/2010/ois_yb_2010.pdf.

349. Ibid., 8–9.

350. Ibid.

351. Ibid.

352. Ibid.

353. Ibid.

354. Ibid.

355. Cuban Adjustment Act, Public Law 89-732, November 2, 1966, www.gpo.gov/fdsys/pkg/STATUTE-80/pdf/STATUTE-80-Pg1161.pdf.

356. Lamrani, *Fidel Castro, Cuba et les États-Unis*, 48–49.

357. Office of Immigration Statistics, "2010 Yearbook of Immigration Statistics."

358. Immigration and Naturalization Services, U.S. Department of Homeland Security, "Estimates of the Unauthorized Immigrant Population Residing in the United States: January 2010," February 2011, http://www.dhs.gov/xlibrary/assets/statistics/publications/ois_ill_pe_2010.pdf.

359. "Salir de Cuba," *El País*, January 15, 2013.

360. Decree-Law no. 302, October 16, 2012, http://www.prensa-latina.cu/Dossiers/ley-migratoria_cuba_2012.pdf.

361. Ibid.; Dirección de Inmigración y Extranjería, "Información útil sobre trámites migratorios," Ministerio de Interior de la República de Cuba, October 2012.

362. Max Lesnik, "Adiós la 'Tarjeta Blanca'," Radio Miami, October 16, 2012.

363. Elizabeth Newhouse, "Disaster Medicine: U.S. Doctors Examine Cuba's Approach," Center for International Policy, July 9, 2012, http://www.ciponline.org/research/html/disaster-medicine-us-doctors-examine-cubas-approach.

364. Decree-Law no. 302.

365. U.S. Department of State, "Cuban Medical Professional Parole Program," January 26, 2009, http://www.state.gov/p/wha/rls/fs/2009/115414.htm.

366. Andrés Martínez Casares, "Cuba Takes Lead Role in Haiti's Cholera Fight," *New York Times*, November 7, 2011.

367. Lamrani, *État de siège: Les sanctions économiques des États-Unis contre Cuba* (Paris: Editions Estrella, 2011).

368. Agence France-Presse, "EEUU saluda flexibilización de la política migratoria en Cuba," October 16, 2012.

369. Juan O. Tamayo, "Cuba cambia las reglas migratorias y elimina el permiso de salida," *El Nuevo Herald*, October 16, 2012.

370. Ruth Ellen Wasem, "Cuban Migration to the United States: Policy and Trends," U.S. Congress, June 2, 2009, http://www.fas.org/sgp/

crs/row/R40566.pdf.

371. *CubaDebate*, "Cuba seguirá apostando por una emigración legal, ordenada y segura," October 25, 2012.

372. Decree-Law no. 302.

373. Max Lesnik, "¿Y los 'Balseros' qué?" Radio Miami, October 16, 2012; *CubaDebate*, "Cuba seguirá apostando por una emigración legal, ordenada y segura."

374. Fernando Ravsberg, "Finalmente llega la reforma migratoria," BBC, October 18, 2012.

375. Michael Parmly, "Spanish Newspaper Reports Impending Reform of GOC," U.S. Interests Section, April 18, 2008, cable 08HAVANA329, http://wikileaks.org/cable/2008/04/08HAVANA329.html.

376. Hugo Llorens, "WHA Assistant Secretary Shannon's Visit to Madrid," American Embassy Madrid, May 9, 2008, cable 08MADRID518, http://wikileaksnor.blogg.no/1292089360_viewing_cable_08madri.html.

377. Richard O. Boyer and Herbert M. Morais, *Labor's Untold Story: The Adventure Story of the Battles, Betrayals and Victories of American Working Men and Women* (New York: United Electrical, Radio and Machine Workers of America, 1955).

Index